THE "M" WORD

(Clearing The Record)

by

Terence Edward Tierney

Bloomington, IN  Milton Keynes, UK

authorHOUSE

AuthorHouse™
1663 Liberty Drive, Suite 200
Bloomington, IN 47403
www.authorhouse.com
Phone: 1-800-839-8640

AuthorHouse™ UK Ltd.
500 Avebury Boulevard
Central Milton Keynes, MK9 2BE
www.authorhouse.co.uk
Phone: 08001974150

First published by AuthorHouse 4/20/2006

ISBN: 1-4259-1328-8 (e)
ISBN: 1-4259-1333-4 (sc)

Library of Congress Control Number: 2006900483
Printed in the United States of America
Bloomington, Indiana

This book is printed on acid-free paper.

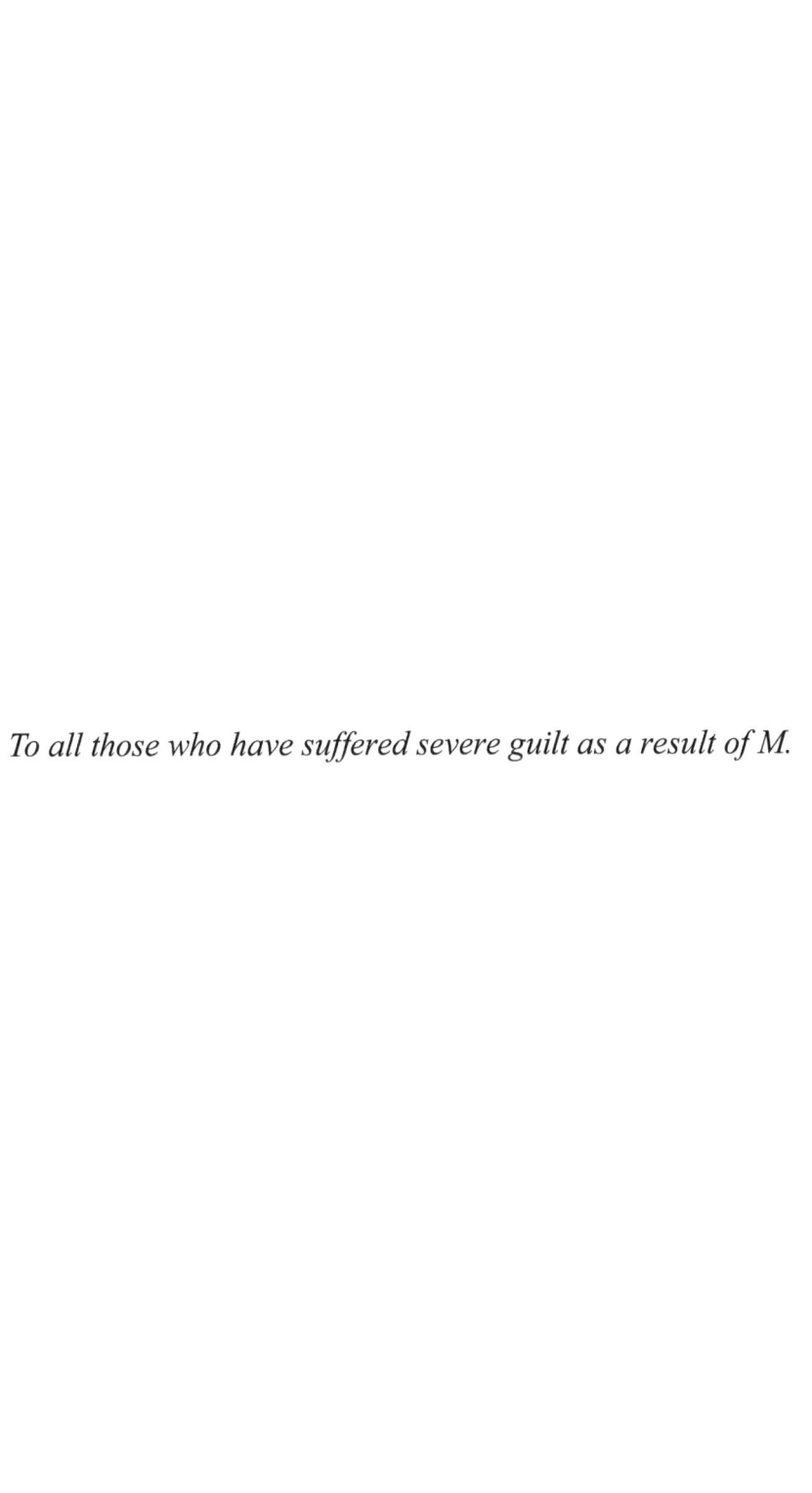

To all those who have suffered severe guilt as a result of M.

Table of Contents

PREFACE   ix

INTRODUCTION   xvii

CHAPTER ONE   Why Do People Masturbate?   1

CHAPTER TWO   The "M" Chapter   12

CHAPTER THREE   "M" Through The Years   22

   PART A - MASTURBATION: THE CHILDHOOD YEARS 22
   PART B - MASTURBATION: THE TEENAGE YEARS   29
   PART C - MASTURBATION: THE "MATURE" YEARS 41

CHAPTER FOUR   "M": Its Physiology and Technique   54

   PART A -   MEN AND MASTURBATION   54
   PART B - WOMEN AND MASTURBATION   72

CHAPTER FIVE   M   To   O: Masturbation: A Tool in Reaching
   Orgasm During Intercourse   86

CHAPTER SIX   A Suggestion For Men and Women   104

CHAPTER SEVEN   Is "M" Ever Preferable to Other Sexual
   Activity?   110

CHAPTER EIGHT   Masturbation: Some Pitfalls and
   Drawbacks   125

EPILOGUE   137

BIBLIOGRAPHY   145

About the Author   153

PREFACE

When I was pondering the idea of this book, I conceived it as a useful tool as well as an informational manuscript. Yet, the more I studied and reflected upon the topic of masturbation, the more I did so with a degree of fear and trepidation. It seems the primary sexual function of humans, masturbation, has become the "Last Frontier" of sexually oriented topics. Indeed, many authors have written about sex: scientists, medical doctors, psychiatrists, psychologists, philosophers, theologians, sex therapists, even novelists. But despite all their study and research, little information on masturbation is available to the general public. Even the most comprehensive scientific and medical studies on sexuality give masturbation short shrift.

With the development of global communication, the Internet and the information highway, we have become, what philosopher Marshall McLuhan predicted, —"A Global Village." In such a world, one would have thought almost everything that needed to be said about sex had already been extensively distributed to the public. However, this is not the case. For alas, good general information on masturbation, and its place in human sexuality, is sorely lacking. So when it dawned on me that this idea for a general book on masturbation might just be a first, I was excited, but uneasy. Never before had a singular work on masturbation, untechnical in nature, with an easily readable format, been placed in the hands of the general public.

Some of my fear about writing this book stemmed from the ingrained mores of societies. Societal conventions implied that so taboo a subject should not be accorded the publicity it so richly deserved. Perhaps, I thought even enlightened publishers would be reluctant, skeptical, and nervous to bring a book on masturbation to print. This was not an unreasonable fear. Witness what the mere mention of masturbation did to Joycelyn Elders, M.D. It brought down a Surgeon General!

We will be taking the position that masturbation is a morally neutral act: not something good; not something bad. It is just a type of sexual behavior that almost everyone has experienced.

The subject of masturbation has been, and to some great extent still remains, a forbidden topic. Even sexually explicit and romantic novels focus almost exclusively upon intercourse. Only hardcore pornography seems to address masturbation, and it does so in a demeaning, exploitative manner devoid of sensitivity. Pornographic or x-rated material places masturbation in a "sexual side show," and this reinforces the twisted notion that masturbation should be relegated to the sexual sewer.

I feel the time has come to raise the curtain on the subject of masturbation and expose it for what it really is— a normal part of the ongoing human sexual experience. My mind and heart tell me that there is a widespread need for information on this subject, since masturbation is an activity that all people experience no matter what their culture, race or creed. It is my conclusion that to continue to leave unexamined and undisseminated knowledge of such universal behavior is a disservice to humanity.

One of the purposes of this book is to dispel the many myths surrounding masturbation, myths which have been perpetuated by societies, and strongly reinforced by various religions. For sixteenth century thought to render masturbation a sexual aberration or a sinful act is understandable. What is not comprehendible is for twentieth century society to continue to perpetuate such an unfounded myth.

Masturbation is not an evil to be condemned but the most basic form of human sexuality—the God-given instinct to find pleasure in an act which is, by its nature, driven toward socialization, and therefore, the continuation of the human species. Masturbation is not a good or goal unto itself, but rather, the basic expression of sexuality which is generally employed when the socialization of sexual expression (a sexual partner) is absent. In adults, it just simply serves to fill in a sexual gap. In children, masturbation is simply a natural exploratory process to discover the potential of their bodies. The discovery of sex through masturbation enables children and teens to cross the threshold into adulthood. Furthermore, sexual knowledge of one's body gained through solitary sex enables adults to enter and sustain a loving sexual relationship with another human being.

Far from being nefarious, as religiously oriented societies have taught, masturbation is one of the most innocuous and natural activities that a human being experiences. Admittedly, masturbation ought not to turn into a selfish act, devoid of sharing the gift of life and love. However, masturbation, per se, is a true expression of human sexuality and should not be condemned out of hand. At length, this solitary act longs to be a social act and we must do whatever possible to aid in its proper transition.

There are those individuals in society who find it sexually stimulating to expose themselves, peep in windows, engage in a sexual fetish, or display some degree of pathological sexual behavior. Most, if not all of these sexual activities, involve masturbation, either during these activities or shortly afterward.

This book is not designed to discuss in detail aberrant sexual behavior, especially with regard to masturbation. Questionable sexual activity is not the focus of this book, and to investigate at length masturbation relative to aberrant behavior would only serve to draw masturbation into a context which, by its nature, is sexually defective. To cast masturbation as an activity of the psychologically impaired could only reinforce the already witless notion that masturbation is somehow at odds with the laws of God and nature. Therefore, while this segment of society masturbates regularly, we here choose to eliminate a commentary on their problem and only focus upon masturbation by human beings understood as normal in behavior.

When reading this book, remember that the value of each individual chapter is in its relationship to the overall presentation of the subject. Viewing each chapter within the context of the entire book allows readers to see a particular aspect of masturbation in relationship to a complete discussion of the topic.

For example, if you are particularly interested in understanding children and masturbation or senior sex and masturbation, it will be absolutely crucial that you view the chapter of special interest within the context of masturbation in general. In this way, you will grasp the true meaning of an individual chapter by understanding that masturbation is natural and universal, and that each age group and social level of sexuality (children, teens, married couples, seniors) bring on different needs, desires and reasons for masturbation.

This book is not intended to be a scientific discussion on the topic of solitary sex, and certainly cannot presume to be a definitive medical or psychiatric treatment on sexual behavior or autoeroticism. (We will leave this duty to scientists.) Rather, my purpose in writing this book is to place in the hands of teachers, religious, counselors, those in the medical and behavioral sciences and especially the average person, an interesting, informative and eminently readable book on a topic in which everyone has some interest, but which is seldom extensively written or spoken about.

I feel this work will be of valuable assistance to those with the unfortunate fate to have contracted the HIV Virus, and those with full-blown AIDS, as well as their counselors, doctors, relatives and friends.

In addition, young adults will benefit from its contents since it provides an overview of a sexual activity most of them experience, while at the same time warning them against the pitfalls of masturbation and its misuse.

Furthermore, I believe that this book will be of great help to senior citizens, males and females in menopause, and especially women who experience difficulty achieving orgasm during intercourse. For seniors, it will assist them in understanding and dealing with the sexual problems brought on by older age, as well as, advice on keeping the sexual organs functioning well. For the menopausal, it can help restore confidence, and perhaps vigor, to their sexual lives and their marriages. For women, I believe this book offers a key answer to the ongoing sexual frustration many experience in their sexual relations with men. After reading it, achieving a climax could be much easier and lots more fun.

I wish this book was a cure-all manual to sexual difficulties, problems and frustrations. Unfortunately, it is not! What I hope to provide here is a guide to understanding ourselves, our personal and religious hangups, and our doubts regarding sexuality and sexual relations.

My intent here is to treat the topic of masturbation in a sensitive manner especially since masturbation is both a delicate yet volatile subject. No matter how you presently feel about masturbation, keep an open mind as to the facts presented herein.

Perhaps upon placing this book down, you will be engulfed by the feeling that you have just been to a place you have seen before but never really understood nor appreciated.

NOTE: Since the title of this book is <u>THE **M**</u> <u>WORD</u>. I have chosen to substitute a capital "**M**" frequently wherever the word masturbation applies.

INTRODUCTION

So Private an Act: A Definition and Commentary

In general terms, masturbation refers to any self-stimulation of the genitals done in a voluntary manner. (If another person stimulates one's genitals against their will, this is not **M**.) Masturbation is a more specific term than autoeroticism, which encompasses any solitary physical or mental sexual activity including masturbation.

Obviously, autoeroticism is too broad a term to describe what we as humans know to be the true experiential meaning of masturbation: namely, any means of self stimulation, the goal of which is to achieve an orgasm.

The term masturbation comes from the Latin verb *masturbari* (which is common or vulgar Latin) and is probably derived from a combination of the Latin words *manus* **(hand),** *turbare* (to disturb), and *stupare* (to defile). Another possibility for its origin is the linking of the Latin noun *mas* (the male seed or semen) and the infinitive verb *turbare* (to disturb). So now we have *manus stupare* (to defile by one's hand) and *mas turbare* (to disturb one's seed). In any event, the common idiom is "to bring oneself or to come to orgasm."

For millenniums, the biblical basis for the explanation of masturbation and its denunciation rested with the text of Genesis 38:8. This passage describes the story of Onan, the son of Judah who was to marry his dead brother's wife and deposit his seed within her. Onan felt the seed ought not to be his. So, when he entered his brother's wife, he withdrew at the last moment and spilled his seed on the ground, whence the Lord, displeased, slew him.

Actually, Onan was not masturbating but simply engaging in a time-honored (if ineffective) form of birth control, *coitus interruptus* (withdrawal).

However, the above represents the beginning of the denunciation of masturbation throughout history. Using religion and the Bible as their foundation, moralistic individuals such as clergymen, doctors, teachers, parents, politicians, kings, etc., took up banners of condemnation, using God's wrath as the fearful incentive to avoid such solitary sex. (Interestingly, in the New Testament, Jesus never mentions **M** and readily forgives adulterers.) By the way, almost everyone who has denounced **M**, has masturbated at some time.

At length, virtually every influential member of society joined in to outline the mental and physical debilities brought on by masturbating. Fear and guilt were the byproducts of such thinking. Children especially were visited with so great a degree of guilt that at times they developed the very fictitious and physical problems that authorities had promised would result from **M**. Adults created an atmosphere of fear and guilt surrounding a normal event, the stage of sexual development we call puberty, which caused emotional and maybe physical problems for teens unconnected with the actual act of masturbating. Moralizing adults attempted to suppress sexual expression, and in so doing, virtually compelled, or at least encouraged, children to engage in **M**.

Masturbation, generally speaking, is not harmful in any way. Scientific and medical studies confirm this fact. Yet, if the person (usually during teen years) believes and feels **M** is evil and despicable (even though it is not), they will develop emotional problems associated with unresolved guilt. These problems are not related to masturbation itself as an act of sexual release.

Fear is the most paralyzing of all emotions. To drill fear into children over an act that nature thrusts upon them is at best wrong and at worst evil and destructive.

No interdisciplinary experts have ever presented any evidence that masturbation is essentially or generally harmful. Yes, there exist many pitfalls and problems brought on by **M**. (We will discuss these later.) However, these represent the exception in overall human experiences.

Masturbation is the ultimate private human act. No action is more individual and isolated except suicide. Thus, solitary sex, as it is commonly understood, is always performed alone and by strict definition excludes a partner. It is, therefore, an experience of total concentration upon oneself. By completely turning in upon oneself and enjoying the experience, a person does run the risk of developing a habit of **M** which can reinforce a degree of introversion. Clearly then, masturbation can become a liability to certain individuals.

<u>Question</u>: Is masturbation a good thing? Answer: No! <u>Question</u>: Is masturbation a bad thing? Answer: No!

Masturbation is neither very good nor very bad. Essentially, it is morally neutral, not an action to be generally recommended—not an action to be universally condemned. There are times when **M** has its place. There are times when **M** is out of place.

M is unique because few important actions in human life are morally neutral. **M** seems to be one of them.

Masturbation doesn't harm oneself and it doesn't hurt others. In certain circumstances, it may benefit the individual. On the one hand, it can be the source of healing certain sexual and marital difficulties, but on the other hand, masturbation can be the source of discord in a sexual relationship, and promote psychological guilt which can lead to low self esteem.

No one has to tell us that masturbation is a word about which no one is suppose to speak. This is an unspoken given in our society. There is virtually a code of silence (the *"Omerta"*) surrounding its very utterance. Simply put, you are not to mention **M** in conversation and writings. If you were to teach a class in sex education, and advised school authorities that you would be speaking extensively on **M**, you would be ushered out of school forthwith.

There exists a mountain of hypocrisy relative to masturbation. Society has told us not to speak of it, yet all medical, scientific and psychological research has long ago definitively agreed that **M** is universal in its presence, and that practically every human being (and many animals) has engaged in it sometime in their lives. In fact, most professional studies suggest that masturbation is a widespread practice in all cultures. The more research that is done, the more it becomes apparent that **M** is extremely prevalent in the teen years, regularly practiced by adults, and is a fairly common activity in one's mature years.

The basic reason given why masturbation is a common practice of the young and senior citizens is that the young have surging hormones which compel them to release sexual tension, and seniors still possess a sexual drive, but frequently not have an active sexual partner Generally, the common denominator for both groups is the lack of a legitimate sexual outlet. The lack of sexual opportunity leads one to seek another avenue of release.

Admittedly, (and regrettably) teens today are having heterosexual sex more often than ever before in history, but still not frequently enough to satisfy their surging hormones. Hence, they masturbate.

Likewise, the sexual feeling and desires of seniors remain present. However, frequently, they have lost their partner through death, disability or divorce, wherefore, there is a need to find a release of sexual tension. Therefore, **M** becomes the safe and viable option if they hope to keep their sexual potency vital.

One of the difficulties researchers on sexual behavior encounter is the reluctance of people to discuss **M** in scientific surveys. People will readily answer questions on intercourse, orgasm, foreplay, birth control, oral sex, etc. Raise the topic of masturbation, and the curtain rings down. Yet, sufficient information is available to legitimately draw many of the forgoing conclusions and observations that indicate the widespread use of masturbation as a sexual outlet.

Religious precepts and societal mores may have placed restraints upon teens and adults in past decades, but not today. And with today's "baby boomer" coming into female/male menopause, together with the complications that the AIDS virus provides in establishing "new" sexual relationships, it is rather obvious that "**M**" will play yet a more prominent role in a person's sexual life as we enter the twenty-first century. Is this a good thing? No, not really. But it is an understandable development.

We will endeavor to treat the subject of **M** from cradle to grave in a compassionate, realistic and non-moral manner. Quite frankly, no one has ever done so in a non-scientific book. We will attempt to place before you most of the information regarding masturbation which has been denied the average person for centuries. We will discuss the pros and cons of **M**, and how **M** relates to children, teens, adults and seniors. We will discuss the reasons persons engage in M; the medical and psychological benefits of **M** in certain circumstances; the pitfalls of **M**; the use of **M** as a tool to help improve a floundering sexual relationship, especially a marriage, and the need to view **M**, not as an evil, but as a neutral activity which carries no moral or psychological penalty if engaged in for the right reasons. **M** is not for excessive physical pleasure but a means to achieve some greater end, the greater end being a satisfying emotional and sexual relationship.

We must smash the taboo surrounding **M**. We must elevate **M**, not to a position of honor, but to a place where it can be understood as an instrument to assist human beings in the establishment of love.

The moralists must be silenced here. All medical and behavioral sciences and their ongoing studies suggest this. Theologians ought to be free to pursue theories which place **M** in its proper perspective without the sword of retribution and ridicule hanging above their heads.

Those who would cross their fingers in a "shame, shame" gesture must be taught to see masturbation not as a good or goal, but the means to allow the proper understanding and use of sex to take its place, not only in society and religion, but in the confines of the human spirit.

God gave human beings the capability to engage in solitary sex, not as an end in itself, but as a means to deal with surging hormones, to release sexual tension without dangerous or illegitimate intercourse, to keep sexual organs healthy and flourishing during the "sunset years." To be sure, God is not in favor of **M**. But He allows humans in the tangle of their minds to find use of it as a tool.

How societies can continuously ignore **M** publicly is a mystery to me. How societies by their silence can ignore one of human nature's most prevalent activities befuddles me. That societies are willing to stigmatize a topic which they refuse to address vexes me.

Dr. David Ruben sums up the subject of **M** most succinctly: "Masturbation is simply a sexual expedient which serves an important purpose. It was the primary sexual activity for most people shortly after they come into the world. It may be their main source of sexual pleasure shortly before they leave this world. In between, if they can arrange it, sexual intercourse is a lot more fun." [David Ruben, M.D., <u>Everything You Wanted to Know About Sex but Were Afraid to Ask</u> (New York, 1971), p. 213.]

CHAPTER ONE

Why Do People Masturbate?

There are as many reasons for masturbation as there are people on this planet. Since as a human activity, masturbation is as individual as it gets, everyone has his or her own particular motivation when it comes to sexual release. My guess is the principal reason why people masturbate will come as no surprise to anyone: it is pleasurable. Quite frankly, it feels good.

Yet apart from the pleasure, there is a battery of other reasons which compel individuals to engage in solitary sex. Some reasons have their roots in a person's psychological makeup. Some reasons can be traced to hormonal surges. Some reasons are linked to a "medical need." And at length, the inherent and intrinsic natural drive to do what is necessary to continue the species compels us to release sexual energy, even if this release is not open to procreation.

As far as pleasure is concerned, we know a primal form of sexual self-pleasuring is experienced by young children. For teens, hormones dictate the drive and frequency of masturbation, and this newfound pleasure can be addictive. As adults, the pleasurable feeling **M** provides is chosen either for itself or to compensate in the absence of a sexual partner.

Masturbation has always been closely associated with the teen years, and rightly so, for the most concentrated masturbatory activity occurs in one's teens. However, the teen years represent a very limited period in a person's life. Clearly, most of a person's life is lived after the teen years have slipped away. Still, **M** continues to be a sexual practice (regularly or occasionally) for most adults well into their golden years.

Why? It is not merely the exploratory experience as in children. It is not "totally" hormonal drive as in teens. It is not absolutely traceable to the lack of a sexual partner as in adults. Why, then, does **M** surface as an experience from cradle to grave? Perhaps it is because the sexual drive we all inherit needs expression— an outlet — no matter what our age.

As people enter adulthood, the option for sexual activity increases. Many heterosexual encounters, a single partner, bisexual affairs, etc., all of these sexual options lessen the need for solitary sex. In adulthood, men and women graduate from the teen "addiction" to **M**, to using **M** as an occasional "fill-in" for dry periods in one's sexual life. Frequently, masturbation becomes a substitute means of sexual fulfillment when heterosexual or homosexual intercourse is not available, when copulation with a partner is impossible or an impractical choice, and when ethical and religious mores coupled with prevailing social standards prohibit or severely discourage purely random sexual behavior. At this point, masturbation or abstinence emerges as the only choices. Abstinence has much to recommend it, but not all people are capable of using abstinence as a means to divert their sexual drive. Moreover, certain physical and psychological needs can override the higher choice of abstinence and compel persons to relieve sexual tension through masturbation.

A good percentage of men and women masturbate simply for pleasure. Perhaps the primary reason humans masturbate for self-gratification is contained in studies where some men and women report that orgasm through **M** is more intense and highly satisfying. In addition, **M** offers a form of sexual independence. Orgasm through **M** is not dependent upon anyone else. It is clean, neat, convenient, and carries no pressure to perform for a partner. Therefore, both sexes, at times, masturbate simply to enjoy their bodies and experience sexual pleasure without the need to satisfy a partner.

Some females find intercourse to be an unsatisfying experience usually due to the absence of orgasm. When orgasm doesn't occur with their husband or partner, women will frequently, so to speak, "take care of themselves." Relative to males, many men choose to masturbate because their female partner is reluctant to have sex often enough to satisfy their frequent need for sexual release. Another reason some people masturbate is to avoid establishing an emotional and sexual relationship. Due to any number of factors, sometimes humans experience and feel a tremendous loss of self-esteem. Lacking self-confidence, they feel uncomfortable with so highly an intimate act as intercourse. These individuals are often compelled to engage in masturbation as their means of sexual release. With **M**, they don't have to be "good in bed," and it allows sexual pleasure and release without human contact. Masturbation can, for these individuals, represent a singular act performed in the absence of another loving partner and can indicate a serious turning inward to oneself. If **M** is practiced regularly and consistently to the exclusion of partners, then **M** becomes a symptom of an underlying personal problem. Undoubtedly, masturbation frees a person from the requirement to become involved in the intimate life of another, while at the same time offering a viable and gratifying sexual outlet. However, this is not a solidly acceptable reason for masturbating. In fact, this behavior can signal the presence of psychological problems. When we engage in sexual activity without the emotional, human contact most sexual activity demands, we invite isolation and court the development of psycho-sexual difficulties.

The above could be linked to maturity. As we mature, we tend to greatly diminish our reliance on **M** (though it still occurs) and continuously search for a sexual partner. Until we find a suitable partner, **M** usually serves as a "stopgap" measure which provides sexual release.

Today, there is yet another particularly nettlesome problem many couples encounter: "The Frequent Flyer Syndrome." This problem revolves around the traveling sexual partner. Being away regularly or frequently can visit a fair amount of sexual frustration upon a marriage or otherwise loving relationship.

In this particular case, sexual experts offer a suggestion.—What happens when you find yourself physically separated for a period of time due to a business trip, while at the same time, experiencing strong sexual desires for your absent partner or mate? You don't just have to merely rely upon or engage in solitary, sex. **M**, absent one's loving partner, is always a hollow experience. Obviously, a long distance relationship is not ideal, but it doesn't need to be completely asexual. John Gray in his book, <u>Mars and Venus in the Bedroom</u> suggests using the telephone to contact your lover and attempt "phone sex." (This is not the 976 variety.)

"Instead of just releasing the sexual tension by masturbating, why not call your partner and have telephone sex? . . . First tell your partner how turned on you are and have how much you wish he or she were there. Ask your partner to touch himself or herself, with eyes closed, as if you were doing the touching. As you touch yourself, imagine your partner touching you. Take turns talking and responding. Describe occasionally how you feel and what you imagine. . . . Eventually, in this way a couple can get to imagining intercourse . . . They can masturbate together. . . ." [John Gray, Ph.D., <u>Mars and Venus in the Bedroom </u>(New York, 1995), p. 125.]

Solitary sex is never the ideal, but in certain situations, by linking up with your partner, you can raise **M** to a higher level. By drawing the one you love into the solitary sex act, you remove feelings of selfishness and raise **M** to a higher plane. In this way, appropriate phone sex has value.

Here are a few additional reasons as to why people masturbate. These can involve a physiological or psychological cause. Interestingly, some people masturbate because it has been recommended to them by a doctor.

Some Medical, Physical and Psychological Reasons for M

We have sound information from medical science that sexual activity can be a source of well being for the entire body. By stimulating many of the body's glands, sexual activity and orgasm help to release a number of hormones into the bloodstream which benefit the body.

In his book, Mars and Venus in the Bedroom. John Gray cites The Power of Fire, a book by Harold Bloomfield, M.D.:

"Regular sex is vital for maintaining higher estrogen levels in women. Higher estrogen has been associated with better bones, better cardiovascular health, and a feeling of joy in life. Men who experience regular sex have a higher testosterone level, which leads to greater confidence, vitality, strength, and energy." (Gray, p. 13.)

In fact, some researchers have suggested that sexual activity regularly releases a form of cortisone, a type of anti-inflammatory hormone. Furthermore, other studies point out that senior citizens who remain sexually active have a somewhat diminished incidence of arthritis. Perhaps the release of certain anti-inflammatory hormones during sexual activity has much to do with this finding. Therefore, **M** among senior citizens can play a role in keeping their sexual organs viable and in good working order while providing overall assistance to the body, at least to some degree.

We are not suggesting that **M** is a cure for any disease or physical discomfort. But rather, only that sexual activity in general seems to help the individual in an overall way. When a sexual partner is lacking, **M** might just be a recommended therapy.

Vascocongestion

This sounds like a foreboding word. But actually, it is a rather simple problem. In fully, sexually aroused males and females, vascocongestion is, of necessity, present. Vascocongestion is the increase of amounts of blood flowing into the tissue of sexual organs and the engorgement of blood vessels in the penis and vaginal area. This is the cause of penile erection and vulva swelling. This biological/physiological occurrence is a prelude to achieving orgasm.

However, there can be times when vascocongestion occurs but orgasm is not or cannot be completed (e.g., someone or something interrupts sexual activity, or it occurs in a public place where one is prevented from relieving oneself, etc.). This congestion of the sex organs without orgasmic relief occurs more frequently in teenagers who arouse quickly and strongly and cannot come to orgasm, but it can and does occur in males and females of all ages. Sometimes when the arousal is so intense and long lasting, the blood almost "refuses to drain" from the penis and vagina. If this condition lasts long enough, pain and discomfort will frequently follow. (Men experience this problem more frequently than women.) The slang terms used to describe this condition in males is "blue balls," "lovers' nuts," et alia. The only quick and effective treatment for this condition is masturbation. (Over-the-counter anti-inflammatory medication can be used but its effectiveness is not always quick and is sometimes nonexistent in low dosages.)

Impotence

Some reasons why masturbation is recommended contain both a psychological and physiological foundation. Impotence in both males and females provides an example of this.

A basic definition of impotence is

"The inability of the male to have or sustain an erection, the lack of which prevents sexual intercourse."

"Chronic impotence in men who otherwise experience erection and ejaculations (e.g., wet dreams or masturbation) almost always has a psychological cause which can only be discovered and eliminated by professional treatment. An occasional inability to have an erection should not be considered impotence. It can usually be attributed to some unfavorable factors in a particular situation. In medical language, the term 'impotence' covers a wide variety of sexual and procreative impediments in men and women." [Erwin J. Goldstein, Ph.D., Martin McBride, M.D. and Will Haeberole, The Sex Book: A Modern Pictorial Encyclopedia (New York, 1971), p. 92.]

There are several causes of physical impotence (e.g., injury, restricted blood flow, etc.), and most of these can be treated successfully. But mental or psychological impotence is much more elusive as to cause, and thus, far more tricky to cure.

Unlike some physical reasons for **M** which include a natural desire for pleasure, relief of vascocongestion, assistance in maintaining healthy, working sex organs during the "golden years," the psychological reasons for **M** are generally more complicated.

In most cases of psychological impotency, internal conflicts, feelings of shame, unresolved guilt, fear et alia are root causes. We know anxiety and depression can diminish sex drive, and taken to the limit, prevent sexual functioning.

In many cases of this form of impotence, masturbation is one of many therapies. Usually, the root cause of malfunctioning is uncovered by a doctor, with masturbation being needed to work a person back into orgasm and sexual activity in general.

Frigidity

Impotence in a female is called frigidity.

The textbook explanation of frigidity is

> "The inability of a woman to experience sexual pleasure or orgasm. The causes of frigidity are mostly psychological. Even women who have a strong desire to love or be loved can suffer from frigidity. However, whether a woman is frigid can be determined only by a professional diagnosis. In this case, professional treatment can usually bring the necessary help. .Sometimes unusual shyness, inexperience, and ignorance in sexual matters are mistaken for frigidity. In such cases, appropriate information and counseling

can alleviate and finally, eliminate the problem. Frigidity and lack of orgasm in women do not mean infertility." (Goldstein, McBride and Haeberole, p. 73.)

Frigidity is a classic form of impotence in females, which can result from ignorance, fear of pregnancy, fear of contracting a disease, and fear due to the experience of rape. All these reasons are understandable, as is any sexual malfunctioning which can be traced to a religious admonition or puritanical upbringing. Many times, masturbation is recommended by professionals to assist a woman who is apprehensive or fearful of sexual activity. Often, people who are psychologically impotent need to "re-learn" how to feel comfortable with sex (a sexual partner), and thus proceed to orgasm. Here, practicing masturbation can play a key role in reestablishing the ability to forge a sexual relationship.

To summarize, there are innumerable reasons for masturbating: virtually as many as there are humans on this planet. Suffice it to say:

> Some masturbate for pure pleasure.
> Some masturbate to assist in a medical problem.
> Some masturbate to learn how to orgasm.
> Some masturbate out of loneliness.
> Some masturbate due to psychological problems.
> Some masturbate to discover their bodies and identities (children).
> Some masturbate because their hormones surge out of control (teens).
> Some masturbate because they are not sexually satisfied by a partner.

Some masturbate because they do not engage in
   intercourse often enough.
Some masturbate to help keep their sexual organs
   alive and functioning (senior citizens).
Some masturbate because they have limited access
   to a sexual
partner (e.g., the blind).

It is a fact that the majority of men and women have two sex lives: one with a partner; one with themselves. They choose to have sex with a partner because it draws into sexual activity the notion of love and emotional sharing. They choose to have sex with themselves because they enjoy it, find **M** physically and sexually intense, and/ or for any of the already outlined reasons. Whatever the reason, a significant number of males and females masturbate throughout their entire lives. Only the frequency varies.

There are explainable, justifiable, and legitimate reasons to engage in masturbation. But remember, not all masturbatory activity is good or helpful, for **M** tends to be a hollow, and at times, a shallow experience. It forever lacks the core beauty of physical, emotional and love-filled sharing. Physical pleasure is fine but only part of the overall equation. Our Creator made us to be copulatory beings and as humans, we require spiritual, emotional, and physical pleasure for complete sexual fulfillment which can only be experienced by sharing our body and souls with someone else.

CHAPTER TWO

The "M" Chapter

It might seem as you read subsequent chapters that a disproportionate amount of space is devoted to women's masturbation practices. This observation is correct. The reason is not that women are more prone to **M** then men; that women have a greater interest in **M**; that women possess an overwhelming need or desire to engage in masturbation. Rather, we will have a stronger focus on female masturbation because **M** for females is more complex. There are numerous variations available to women for masturbating which men are not accorded. A great deal of these variations is directly related to the anatomy of a woman. In females, techniques of masturbation vary considerably. Yet, one golden thread emerges linking virtually all women: sooner or later, in one way or another, clitoral stimulation is required. Despite the plethora of literature available on the subject of sex, men continue to fail their sexual partners in the key areas women need in order to be sexually responsive and fulfilled: emotion, romance, and demonstrative love. Oh yes, as we approach the third millennium, men still do not appreciate nor understand the nature of a woman's body.

A woman will usually not come to an orgasm with a man if the sexual activity is based upon physical stimulation alone. (It is a well-established fact that most prostitutes never orgasm with their clients, with high-priced call girls being the possible exception.) The absence of emotional stimulation can result in a lack of adequate physical stimulation, no matter how deliberate the foreplay.

Women desire an orgasm in an atmosphere which it is not filled with pressure or expectation. They want to feel relaxed, emotionally involved in body, mind and heart. A good climax can't be rushed. Often, only solitary sex fills the bill.

We hope to show during our subsequent discussions throughout the remaining chapters of this book that with loving "teamwork," orgasm together (not simultaneously) is a real possibility on virtually every occasion.

Before we proceed any further, let's summarize what researchers have already established concerning **M** as follows:

> That both males and females engage in **M.**
> That very young children engage in **M.**
> That teens engage in **M.**
> That adult men and women engage in **M.**
> That senior citizens engage in **M.**
> That single males engage in **M.**
> That single females engage in **M.**
> That people engage in **M** regardless of their social status or religious creed.
> That virtually every human person who has ever-lived at some time engaged in **M.**
> That young children masturbate because it represents a process of discovery and development.
> That teens masturbate because raging hormones "force" them into **M** as their bodies change from a child to an adult.
> That singles masturbate for lack of a regular partner.

That married males masturbate because the female does not accord the male the frequency of intercourse he desires.

That married females masturbate because the male frequently fails to provide the quality of sex that the female desires to relieve sexual frustration.

That senior citizens masturbate, primarily due to the fact that their partner has given up on sex, they are ill or disabled, or they find themselves single again as a result of divorce or the death of their partner.

Furthermore, we know that it has been long established that **M** is a universal activity. While we may have discovered cultural variations, that masturbation is almost as common as sexual intercourse is an anthropological fact.

Consider for a moment a recent survey of young women in 29 countries conducted by <u>Cosmopolitan Magazine</u>. The results published in the March 1996 issue reaffirm the universality of masturbation. Some of these results on **M** are as follows: 75.6% of those responding to the survey said they engaged in masturbation. The frequency of **M** varied by country. The United Kingdom led all countries that responded with the greatest percentage of women who masturbate frequently, 30.4%. The United States came in second with 28.5% of the respondents saying they masturbate frequently. Interestingly, Portuguese women masturbated with the least frequency.

In the overall category of masturbation, Japan was "Numero Uno." From those Japanese women responding, 11.3% said they masturbate frequently, while 80.3% do so occasionally. Taken together, 91.6% of Japanese respondents acknowledge that they masturbate. While

I don't rely much on percentages, these numbers are unmistakable. People all over the world masturbate!

M is a documented sexual practice in most cultures from ancient to modern times. The Europeans appear to practice masturbation as often and in much the same way as Americans. As a matter of fact, Europeans may even be more apt to masturbate owing to their more liberal approach to sex in general. This is not to say that every European country encourages **M**. France, for instance, would be more liberal: Ireland, more conservative. We know Sweden is very open regarding sexual matters, while other European countries prefer that sexual matters remain somewhat private.

We know, as far as the ancients are concerned, that masturbation was practiced by the Greeks and Romans, the Egyptians and Babylonians, the Hebrews, and others. It appears that some civilizations praised the practice of **M**, while others condemned it.

Researchers tell us that the Egyptians were among the first to fashion a dildo (which is an artificial form of a penis). Examples of dildos have been discovered within the tombs of Ancient Egyptian burial grounds. Hence, we can conclude that **M** was a common activity among Egyptian women. And, if in fact women of ancient times engaged in **M**, then we can logically surmise that ancient males also found **M** a comfortable, sexual outlet. Indeed, references to employing various objects to pleasure oneself can even be found in biblical literature.

We know that **M** was a widespread practice during medieval times. The denunciation of masturbation by medieval theologians, at the very least, confirms this fact. In those days, a certain penance was prescribed by the priest for engaging in **M**. Clearly then, **M** was so common an activity, that the Catholic Church saw fit to include the practice of masturbation in its Penitentials (books with prescribed or specific penances for specific sins).

As an aside, during the Crusades when men went off to 'Tight the heathen," many required their wives to wear a chastity belt for the duration of their absence. This belt was made of iron and chain, and covered the vaginal area with a type of metal cage containing small slots. A chain secured it about the waist and between the legs. The chains were ultimately secured by a padlock. The slots allowed for urination but not penetration (even with hand or fingers), thus insuring a husband/soldier the comfort of knowing that his wife would be safe and faithful to him. This chastity belt was so awkward and uncomfortable that even **M** was virtually an impossible alternative. (By the way, he took the only key to the padlock with him on his crusade.) One wonders what happened if the husband managed to get himself killed.

We do not intend to belabor the history or universality of masturbation. The foregoing gives you, the reader, a brief idea of the longevity of **M** as a sexual practice, and the "comfort" to know that virtually everyone, everywhere, at all times in history and culture, somehow engaged in solitary sex.

Here is a curiosity for us: Masturbation by animals.

Just so we humans don't feel alone in the act of masturbation, ponder this thought: animals masturbate too. Anthropologists, zoologists, naturalists and others have observed and documented self-stimulation among animals.

You might well imagine that sexual activity akin to humans has been observed among the primates: apes, monkeys, chimpanzees, etc. But even what we call sub-primates such as cats, dogs, and deer engage in sexual arousal and masturbation.

It seems that males of various animal species engage in self-stimulation, even to the point of orgasm. However, it is more difficult for observers to document orgasmic activity in the female of animal species.

The prevalence of **M** among male animals can be witnessed more easily. Most males can be seen with an erection, and many have been witnessed to "the shooting out of their seed." Unfortunately, as with humans, female animals offer no clear-cut sign of orgasm. The male primates manipulate their penises much the same as human males using hands or rubbing their gentiles against some object such as the ground, rocks, trees etc. Female primates stimulate themselves by rubbing their vulva area against various objects and by touching themselves with their hand.

Masturbatory activity in primates is less frequent for females than males. And in the sub-primates, the female rarely appears to masturbate. Furthermore, masturbatory activity occurs both inside and outside captivity.

Some of the animals which have been observed to masturbate are:

apes
chimpanzees
Rheus monkeys
porcupines
cats
dogs
elephants
dolphins
rats
rabbits
horses
bulls
deer

The following represents two scientifically observed descriptions of **M** engaged in by animals. One is the male red deer, and the other, a female chimpanzee. These observations were reported by C.S. Ford and F.A. Beach in their book, <u>Patterns of Sexual Behavior</u> (New York, 1951), at p.161 and p.163. Speaking of the sexual activity of the red deer,

"The act is accomplished by lowering the head and gently drawing the tips of the antler to and fro through the herbage. Erection and extrusion of the penis from the sheath follow in five to seven seconds. There is but little protrusion and retraction of the penis and no oscillating movement of the pelvis. Ejaculation follows about five seconds after the penis is erected, so that the whole act takes ten to fifteen seconds. . ."

"Adult female apes sometime devote considerable energy and ingenuity to the achievement of vulval stimulation. In one instance, a full-grown chimpanzee was playing with a mango. First she placed the fruit upon her external genitals. Then, apparently dissatisfied with the results of this procedure, the animal put the mango on the floor, sat down on it, turning, twisting, and rubbing awkwardly with her hands and continually varying her position. . . Subsequently, the chimpanzee raised and lowered her body repeatedly, bumping her genitals against the fruit. Later, she explored the vagina with a finger. . ."

What can we conclude from the observation of **M** in animals? Namely, that **M** is even more universal in its nature and use than most anyone could imagine. The history of higher animal life itself (Remember, humans are animals.) is also the history of masturbation as a sexual activity.

A Concluding Commentary

The desire for sex is very much alive in most peoples from childhood to old age. This represents a natural drive. We all by nature desire a partner with whom to share our bodies and souls.

When we are without a partner for any number of reasons, we turn to ourselves to provide a sexual outlet until we discover that "someone." It is amazing to me that since **M** is so universal in all cultures and creeds, that we so very seldom speak to **M** as an important issue regarding human sexuality. To a great extent, we all know why this is so—masturbation is **taboo!**

This is truly an enigma! Since virtually everyone has engaged in masturbation, it seems almost hypocritical that the act of M, so universal in practice has few authors writing extensively about it. It would appear that sex without a partner is not accepted as society's norm, so society and most religions condemn it out of hand. However, despite what the "pillars" of society and religion tell us about solitary sex, masturbation is and remains normal human activity. In fact, **M** is clearly a norm in societal behavior: more people masturbate than engage in sexual intercourse. To be sure, **M** is not a goal to be sought after of itself, but a tool to be used effectively as we wait to find a loving partner, and perhaps build a family, which represents the cornerstone of society.

CHAPTER THREE

"M" Through The Years
Part A - Masturbation: The Childhood Years

Part B - Masturbation: The Teen Years

Part C - Masturbation: The "Mature" Years

PART A - MASTURBATION: THE CHILDHOOD YEARS

It is a given that one of the most fulfilling experiences of human life is the birth of one's child. The parents are rightfully ecstatic, and the joy of holding your child for the first time is unexcelled. This new baby is so beautiful; so precious a gift; so fragile; so innocent; so vulnerable; so lovable that it seems almost obscene to think that such a tiny life could soon begin to masturbate.

This chapter may shock some readers when they discover that baby Jane or baby John may actually masturbate as infants and continue throughout their lives.

There appears to be no dispute among the experts in medicine and the social and behavioral sciences that sexuality begins at birth, (Some would say earlier.), and develops throughout life along with other bodily functions. This development of sexuality is not absolutely orderly in its progression so as to say every child reaches this or that stage at a particular time. Reproductive development is easier to document and monitor.—Psycho-sexual development is not.

We know that infants of both sexes have been observed to be sexually aroused even to the point of having achieved a form of orgasm. These observations are of a limited nature, since most people doing the observing are parents or guardians who are not looking for signs of sexual arousal, or fail to recognize this behavior when it manifests itself. In fact, since few people really understand that sexual behavior is possible in their infants, they would never notice any signs of such arousal unless these signs were truly overt, and thus obvious.

All children develop a sexual behavior, and nature refines it as they mature. Some children exhibit sexual responses in the early months of life. Others do not. Available data supports the premise that no specific age for sexual responsiveness can be established with any degree of certainty. Furthermore, it would appear that boys are more likely to engage in some form of sex play while in childhood. However, since erections are easily observed in males, we can gather a body of scientific data. On the other hand, we know far less regarding observable sexual arousal in female children due to a decided lack of verifiable indications. (It is possible that the same degree of sex play is common to both boys and girls.) But let us look at a rare example of masturbation by a young female child. The following is a descriptive example, supplied by a mother, who observed her three-year-old daughter masturbating.

"Lying face down on the bed, with her knees drawn up, she started rhythmic pelvic thrusts, about one second apart. These thrusts were primarily pelvic, with the legs tensed in a fixed position. The forward components of the thrusts were in a smooth and perfect rhythm which was unbroken except for momentary pauses during which the genitalia were readjusted against the doll on which they were pressed; the return from each thrust was convulsive, jerky. There were 44 thrusts in unbroken rhythm, a slight momentary pause, then 10 thrusts, and then a cessation of all movement. There was marked concentration and intense breathing with abrupt jerks as orgasm approached. She was completely oblivious to everything . . . There was a noticeable relief and relaxation after orgasm." [A.C. Kinsey et al. Sexual Behavior in the Human Female (Philadelphia, 1953), pp. 104-105.]

While most parents or guardians will probably say they never saw their very young children do anything like that which is described above, the fact is many children do engage in **M**. Quite frankly, most adults simply fail to see any sexual significance to the actions of very young children which explains why they never really observe the youngster masturbating. Parents and guardians are inclined to ignore or "brush-off" the young child's movements, moans, and heavy breathing during their self-stimulation.

However, as the child grows older (5-6-7-8 years old) many parents do observe these young ones touching themselves. The common reaction, at least by most American parents, is to admonish their children, scold them, and tell them that they "must not do that again." This reaction is directly attributable to the social taboo associated with "playing with oneself and the religious precepts against masturbation. So strong is this taboo that occasionally some parents or guardians, upon witnessing a child masturbating, are driven to extreme and unconscionable behavior.

An example of this attitude can be found in a recent Pennsylvania case in which an eight-year-old child (a girl) is observed by her foster parents to be obviously masturbating. These foster parents were so outraged by this simple childhood act that they threw boiling water on the child's body and genitals, and placed hot red pepper in her vagina to punish her for what they considered to be a despicable action.

The tragedy here is child abuse, pure and simple. (The parents were arrested. Happily, the child recovered.) But the cause of their outrage is linked to a terrible misunderstanding of **M** and sexuality in general. Yes, these two people were probably child abusers in the past who have a pathological problem or illness. However, in the described incident, **M** triggered the abusive behavior. They could not understand nor tolerate a child masturbating. Alas, ignorance breeds fear, and ultimately, irrationality and violence.

The above account is but one profound example which argues to the need for a book on masturbation. Knowledge is power and it helps us to avoid overreacting to a situation or action we do not fully understand. We must once and forever dispel the myth that **M** is evil. I believe that masturbation is not an evil act in God's eyes, and it ought not to be viewed as wrong in society's eyes. **M** is essentially a morally neutral activity.

The accounting of this tragic story just serves to prove how ignorant some people can be regarding childhood sexual development. To many people, perhaps even most people, it may be surprising to discover that small children actually masturbate. But we must learn that human beings are sexual beings from womb to tomb.

You might ask the question, "Why do children so very young begin to masturbate?" Quite simply, the answer is, "it feels good." The child, whether male or female, feels sensations when private parts are bathed. Cleansing of the genitals by gentle rubbing creates sexual sensations, and very soon the child learns that he or she can do the same. Most experts agree that it is common by age three that a pattern of **M** is established. It appears that self-exploration (common among youngsters) leads to self-manipulation which is a common form of sex play as the child progresses in age. To a certain extent, this pattern of sexual play continues until the onset of puberty.

Although very young boys fondle and manually stimulate their penises on a regular basis, they infrequently carry this through to "orgasm." In the case of very young girls, they are more prone to stimulate themselves by rhythmic movement of the lower body. A large degree of self-stimulation by very young children is the result of curiosity rather than a conscious act or effort at sexual arousal. The fact is, most children discover erotic pleasure from their sexual organs by touching themselves or as a result of rubbing against objects while playing. (This is particularly true of young girls.)

"A little girl becomes sexually aroused while climbing a rope, riding a bicycle or pressing herself against a mattress. She does not understand the significance of this novel feeling but as it is pleasant, she tries to elicit it again, and this time she uses her hands. One day she carries the activity far enough to experience orgasm; she has now learned to masturbate. The pleasure thus obtained, positively reinforces the activity and it may become habitual." [Herant A. Katchadourian and Donald T. Lunde, Fundamentals of Human Sexuality (New York, 1972), pp. 198-199]

Most evidence suggests that the approximate starting time for the actual and deliberate engagement of masturbation in children is between ten and twelve years of age for boys and between seven and ten years of age for girls. It appears that the onset of conscious M rarely begins later. Some time after a child reaches the age often, masturbation generally becomes a more specifically conscious activity, with boys masturbating to orgasm and ejaculation and girls to a female climax.

Everybody seems to be aware of sexual activity among teens, young adults, and mature adults. But few appreciate nor understand the profound sexual activity of younger children. In society, we simply do not view this age group as sexually active, especially in regard to masturbation. The thought of a youngster masturbating just does not cross our minds. Actually, it is a uniformly uncomfortable thought for most of us when it does cross our minds.

In summary, a child explores his or her own body during the course of growing up. Sometimes this exploration takes the form of fondling the genitals, which is the beginning of M. Like all of us, a child will tend to repeat activity which results in good feeling and pleasure. As the child moves closer to puberty, their sexuality becomes more insistent. With the actual arrival of puberty, sexual feeling (physical and mental) takes on a new and higher dimension. Now reproduction is possible, and sexual feeling can be sought out as a pleasure unto itself, not merely a good feeling when one touches private parts. The sexual consciousness which emerges in youth will grow and develop until they fully understand the power and pleasure which nature has provided for them. Then, and only then, can the sexual drive be directed and channeled toward an object of love. **M** is an outlet. But sexual desire must sooner or later, in one way or another, be socialized.—**M** must become less important, while sharing one's body with another in love, more important.

So to any parents or guardians reading this section, be kind, patient, and understanding of the sexual drives of your child. You experienced these same drives but have forgotten. Know that your child is not perverted, evil, odd or "sick" if you happen upon him or her in the act of masturbating. What they are actually doing is growing up sexually. They seek, unconsciously, to discover the mysteries of their body and the hidden pleasure God has seen fit to bestow upon all of us.

PART B - MASTURBATION: THE TEENAGE YEARS

Puberty, that monumental period of physical, psychological, and emotional change, is one of the most difficult and confusing times in a person's life. It is a difficult time for an adolescent because the bodily changes associated with puberty strike a teen somewhat suddenly. Hormones begin to flow and surge throughout their bodies. The sexual organs begin to change in size and shape. Their alterations include the enlargement of the penis in males and the appearance of recognizable breasts in females. In addition, pubic hair begins to grow around the genitals, while hair under the arms, and on the legs, arms, and face start to surface. Frequently, a spurt in height accompanies this stage of growth, and in males, increasing strength in muscular tissue becomes apparent. For females, puberty signals the onset of menarche or their first period. Puberty is quite simply the time when boys become more masculine and girls become more feminine; a boy becomes a "man" and a girl becomes a "woman."

However, it is well for us to remember that puberty and adolescence are not specific points in time but ongoing processes of growth and development which cover an extended period of time.

Puberty ushers in the capacity to reproduce the species and the ability to engage in sexual intercourse. However, we must be aware of the fact that reproductive capacity (fertility) and sexual ability or responsiveness (potency) are not identical. These are separate and distinct functions and can occur on different schedules during sexual development. For instance, just because a girl experiences first menarche, it does not mean she can instantly conceive a child; just because a boy experiences initial ejaculation, it does not mean sufficient sperm are present to impregnate a female. Initially, both girls and boys are able to engage in intercourse but unable to reproduce an offspring. Generally, a certain period of time is necessary for the proper hormones to do their work: allow the egg to properly implant on the womb; allow the production of sperm to achieve a level necessary (number of sperm) to successfully reach and fertilize the female egg. No one knows the exact time frame for initial fertility, but it is rather short.

As puberty progresses, surges in sexual feelings and the emotional development of a degree of preoccupation with sexual matters emerge. During this period, girls begin to become interested in boys and boys start to look at girls in a new way. Thus, the heterosexual attraction begins to take root. For the first time in their lives, boys and girls desire to interact. (E.g., Boys no longer regard talking and associating with girls to be a "sissy thing.")

Puberty also brings on another important experience—orgasm! As we have previously discussed, prior to puberty, masturbation by children meant simply touching themselves to elicit pleasurable feelings and sometimes a "weak" orgasm. Now **M** means true orgasm: the pleasant feeling turns into an ecstatic feeling.

There is, however, an element in sexual development that is lacking at this time of puberty and adolescence: the full emotional capacity for sexual love. During the initial stages of puberty, a teen can give birth to a child or father a child, and still lack the fundamental understanding of what sexual intercourse actually means: a physical, emotional and spiritual union of two minds, hearts, and souls.

Masturbation by Young Females

The first real sign of conscious masturbation in females usually occurs between the ages of seven and ten. At this point, young girls begin to touch and explore their genitals more thoroughly. They begin to discover a good sexual feeling which can be repeatedly enjoyed.

In young females, overall sexual development is somewhat slower than in young males. While physically, girls achieve menarche (their first period) at an earlier age than boys experience their first ejaculation, they are slower to develop sexual responsive behavior. Boys experience a more sudden urge to be sexually active. Girls tend to build to sexual activity over a period of years, the tragedy of young teen pregnancy notwithstanding.

Since girls explore their sexual feelings more gradually than boys, they tend to experience fewer orgasms during the early stages of puberty. Therefore, they generally do not masturbate as often. Girls begin to experience stronger sexual feelings as puberty progresses but genital arousal does not descend upon them with the same intensity as it does with boys. At this point in female sexual development, young girls have a greater awareness of the swelling of the labia and the erection of the clitoris during sexual arousal. But unlike young boys, girls are less likely to vigorously pursue the physical sensations. Also, at this stage of development, girls are more reluctant to discuss, even with their peers, the purely physical feelings associated with sexual arousal.

As puberty progresses, a young female begins to experience a "crush" over a certain boy, and closer contact with the opposite sex becomes desirable. She wants to be with and talk to boys. But purely physical contact is not uppermost in her mind. What is happening here is the early stage of socialized "sexual" behavior.

As females at this age become more aware of their bodies, they begin to act upon the experience of sexual arousal and will bring themselves to a climax at least occasionally. However, unlike boys at this age, girls generally do not become involved in group masturbation or perform mutual **M** with a close friend. Among young females, this type of sexual activity is not a common occurrence.

[In the later stages of sexual development, girls will learn to play at sex for love and boys will learn to play at love for sex.]

Girls are more apt to begin regularly enjoying **M** when they approach their mid-teens. Most do so by fondling themselves and gently stroking the pubic area. Soon, the clitoris becomes erect and the labia fill with blood to the point of swelling. With continued stimulation and added pressure, orgasm usually follows quickly. The clitoris is the organ which is at the center of sexual satisfaction and gratification. It can be stimulated directly with a finger or indirectly with leg or thigh pressure. Either way, once teens learn to orgasm, they find ways to do it often.

When it comes to masturbation, girls have a distinct advantage over boys. Females leave no telltale sign of the action or the pleasure that results from orgasm. Unlike boys who must make certain the semen is "collected" or removed, most girls can quietly masturbate anywhere, at any time.

How do girls achieve an orgasm virtually undetected? They can use thigh pressure. By simply crossing their legs and rubbing their thighs together while applying gentle but firm pressure to the labia and clitoris, females can stimulate their genitals and orchestrate the pleasure to its peak. If they can avoid gasping and moaning at the point of climax, no one except the most observant will be able to tell orgasm has occurred.

Young girls can also orgasm quietly using their fingers to stimulate the genitals while covering their lap with a sweater or coat but this approach is not nearly as clandestine.

When speaking of **M** in females, we must note that the average girl masturbates by touching the genitals directly or by imitating the action of intercourse through the insertion of their fingers into the vagina. (A much smaller number use thigh pressure.) Fingers are usually employed to gently knead the pubic area (the entire vagina - labia, the pubic mons, the area surrounding the clitoris and the clitoris itself). Like young boys, girls do not have to be taught to masturbate. Nature allows them to discover this sexual activity on their own.

Once a young girl becomes acutely aware of her pubic area, and discovers the sensitivity of her inner thighs and vagina, the good feeling this exploration provides, leads her to reproduce the pleasurable sensation again and again through masturbation.

Masturbation by Young Males

Just as with young girls, young boys begin to experience some form of sexual arousal and perform acts of self-stimulation from the earliest years of life. In general, the first true signs of conscious masturbation in males usually occur after the age of ten. They begin to explore their bodies and sexual feelings with a purpose in mind.

Males, early on in puberty, begin to masturbate on a regular basis. They have sexual thoughts and experience sexual feelings and arousal, but the initial fondling and playing with themselves result in a "dry orgasm" with seminal fluid absent. This initial orgasm lacks the complete experience of ejaculation. As they proceed further into puberty and develop sexually, sperm is produced and the various seminal secretions present themselves. Now the experience of orgasm is complete—full sensation and lots of fluid.

The first experience of ejaculation for males usually occurs in one of two ways. Either they awake during a sexual dream and discover a mucous-like liquid squirting from the penis, or they find themselves "wet" upon awakening in the morning. This experience can be unsettling to a young boy because he knows something different is happening to his body, but frequently, he can't understand it to his satisfaction. Soon, however, during conscious sexual arousal, a young male learns to touch his penis, move it about and carry this fondling through to ejaculation. The actual technique of **M** for a boy is rather simple. Either he strokes the penis with his hand to the point of ejaculation, or he rubs the penis against an object such as a mattress.

Since preteens and early teens are very much group conscious and group oriented, some sexual experiences tend to occur in this context. These sexual experiences can include exposing themselves to each other; touching each other; group **M**. However, it must be understood that more than mere sexual interest is at work here. Certain social and psychological needs are present.

Unlike girls, boys take part in group or mutual masturbation. Sometimes they even challenge each other as to: "Who has the biggest penis?" "Who can come the quickest?" "Who can shoot the farthest?" This group experience can lead to a more private experience. For example, two of the boys might decide to touch each other when they are in a more private setting. They masturbate each other to orgasm.

We must note here that these above-mentioned experiences are not in and of themselves abnormal, but rather, the result of tremendous sexual tension brought on by surging hormones and social and emotional needs. This sexual activity is not a prelude to homosexuality, but a rather common experience of males during puberty when erections are continuous and relentless. The urge to masturbate is so great among teen males that they can barely resist the temptation to bring themselves to orgasm.

Most of the time, **M** is accompanied by sexual fantasies. Actually, fantasizing is very common for both sexes during this period of sexual development. Daydreaming is a classic "occupation" of teens, and whether at home or in school, many daydreams are sexual in nature. Teenagers think about sex a great deal and touch themselves often. It almost "defines" what it means to be an adolescent.

Today, teenagers tend to be very sexually active, a truly regrettable development within an "enlightened society." Adolescents fail to understand, and are ill-equipped to comprehend, the consequences of their actions: the responsibility and emotional upheaval brought on by pregnancy; the possibility that they can contract a sexually transmitted disease; and the final horror of discovering that they are HIV positive or have full-blown AIDS. Society has allowed its young to enter and experience the adult world of sex without the proper education which should include admonitions and restraints. In fact, societies encourage sexual activity in young teens through the media, movies, music, books, magazines, plays, dress etc., which propels them into a sexual world that is far too complicated for them to appreciate. (Intercourse is an extremely emotional and sacred act which even many adults fail to comprehend.)

Be that as it may, teenagers experiment with intercourse. Yet, even though as many as 60 to 70% of all teens have experienced intercourse by age nineteen, these teens continue to masturbate just as their predecessors in human history. **M** is as prevalent today as it was fifty - one hundred - two hundred - one thousand years ago. Teenage masturbation is still a natural and readily available sexual outlet. It appears to matter little that today's teens have the sexual outlet of intercourse available to them which other generations did not due to the constraints of society. **M** is still, and will remain, the big sexual word in their vocabulary. Just because boys are more insistent and girls are more willing does not mean that today's youth masturbate less. On the contrary, they masturbate as much, if not more, than previous generations.

Far from being viewed as an evil, or even a despicable act, masturbation must be seen as a normal and natural way of introducing the beauty and power of sex to a naive group.

To parents and guardians we say, children and teenagers should not be scolded or chastised for masturbating as long as it is not done in public. **M** is perfectly acceptable private behavior, and is one topic which must be discussed with your teens. They should know clearly that **M** is not something good and it is not something bad. Rather, masturbation represents an innate transitory experience which, if viewed properly, can assist in wholesome sexual development.

As parents or guardians, you need not be concerned if your teenagers masturbate. You might want to discourage any overuse of this sexual outlet, but teens ought not to be made to feel guilty because they perform a sexual activity that is almost physically and psychologically impossible to avoid for their age group.

The best approach to teenage **M** is to downplay it. The only time that your teen's masturbating should cause you concern is if you have firm, clear, evidence that your teen is masturbating excessively. If you know for certain that your teenager is masturbating two, three, four times a day, every day, then his or her **M** is signaling a deeper developmental and emotional problem. The act of masturbation is not the problem. It is only a symptom of underlying psychological difficulties which call for counseling.

If you are truly concerned about the sexual behavior of your teenager(s), forget about **M**. Your energies must be directed to doing all you can to avoid having your teens engage in sexual intercourse. Apart from drug use, random sexual activity poses the greatest threat to teens and their families. With the possibility of pregnancy and/or the contraction of a sexually transmitted disease, sexual intercourse among teens is a highly dangerous activity. The emotional and physical devastation, which can result from an active and random sexual life, is both individual and social. In light of this knowledge, masturbation is truly a very harmless activity

Since this book is about masturbation, it is important that I offer some concluding remarks regarding adolescence and masturbation.

The adolescent period carries a degree of self-centeredness with it. A preoccupation with one's body and emotions, coupled with individual interests and activities, characterizes the teen years. To an extent, teens live in a world of their own. They frequently shut out adults from their thoughts and inner feelings. To a great degree, teens desire to "go it alone" when it comes to taking guidance from others, yet crave the social contact and acceptance of their peers. Adolescence is a period of transition from childhood. How a teen copes with this somewhat volatile time in their lives can determine how their adulthood will be lived out.

The sexual transition which takes place during the adolescent years plays a major role in future sexual relationships. **M** is nature's way of introducing teens to the pleasure of the human body and assists them in understanding the power of sex. Adulthood will usher in an even more complicated period in our sex life: the socialization of sexual behavior. Masturbation, that insistent, primary release of sexual power for teens, will begin to become a "secondary" sexual activity having given way to the many options and experiences of adult sexuality. However, **M** will most probably remain an active part in the sexual lives of adults until death. But once a person is fully mature (physically and sexually), it becomes necessary for **M** to take second place.

However, for teens, adulthood has not yet arrived. Therefore, it is imperative for us to speak openly and honestly to teens about their primary sexual outlet: masturbation. Unfortunately, addressing the topic of **M** still makes many people very uncomfortable, and spawns a variety of ignorant and outrageous reactions.

One such scenario took place in the early 90's. It was a sad day in America when Joycelyn Elders, M.D. was forced to resign as Surgeon General of the United States over remarks she made regarding masturbation with a view to sex education. Many people, including the very educated, accused her of suggesting that sex education programs teach students how to masturbate. Firstly, Dr. Elders did not suggest that teens be instructed on how to masturbate. Secondly, no one has to _teach_ teens how to masturbate. They already do so regularly.

The response to Dr. Elder's words was telling. Masturbation is still a _taboo_ word to utter, even though most Americans masturbate. Many people in society are not willing to recognize their own ignorance in the matter of **M**. For an individual, especially a highly respected physician, to be roundly denounced by simply speaking about masturbation indicates that religious moralism and societal ignorance are still very much present in our age of liberation, and enlightenment. As parents, guardians, teachers, and counselors, we must resist this moralism and speak out courageously and thoughtfully to every teenager about masturbation and its rightful place in human evolution and in our lives.

PART C - MASTURBATION: THE "MATURE" YEARS

[Note: For the purpose of this section, we will be applying the term mature "broadly" to encompass all people over the age of fifty.]

Americans have always placed a premium on the benefits of youth and youthfulness, especially with regard to sexual matters. As a matter of fact, American society virtually defines sexual prowess and performance in terms of "being" and "looking" young. We need to search no further than our television sets, our music videos, and the plethora of multimedia advertisements to sample the subtle (and not so subtle) emphasis placed upon sex, sexuality and youthfulness: we exercise not only to be healthier but to look younger; we color our hair and cream our faces to ward off the effects of aging; we choose to dress in a manner which makes us more sexually attractive. To sing the praises of youthfulness and sexuality is understandable. But let us not forget two important points: One, that the American population is aging rapidly. Two, that sexuality, sexual interest, and sexual performance have never been the sole provinces of youth. Seldom do we think of older Americans as sexually active. The fact is, sex is alive and well among our mature population.

"Mature" adults, as with all age groups, masturbate. **M** in one's later years may not be as frequent a sexual exercise as in one's youth but it is nonetheless present in the senior population. In fact, **M** can become a necessary therapeutic exercise as the aging process begins to take its toll on a person's sexual organs. As long as the sexual organs are in good working order, **M** will have a place in a person's overall sexual life. Let us discuss for a few pages, sex in the mature years and the role masturbation plays in helping maintain an active sex life.

One of the great glories of science and medicine is that they help provide ways to keep us living longer year after year. For centuries, the life expectancy of men and women has been on the rise. New developments in medicine, pharmacology and the behavioral sciences have provided human beings the benefit of living longer, healthier lives. This progression in longevity has allowed many people to further contribute their knowledge, experience, creativity, and philosophy to civilization. Generation after generation grow, develop, and flourish as more of its people live well into old age. But as with any other facet of human life, age can bring on its own set of problems and obstacles.

When human life, as we know it, began thousands of years ago, men and women were very lucky to live to age forty. If disease and starvation didn't kill them, predators did them in. (This sounds almost like today.) So God in His infinite wisdom gave nature the job of seeing to it that human life continued on so as to insure the survival of the human species.

Since most women, and virtually every man, died with their reproductive capabilities still in place, annoyances like menopause didn't exist. But as we discovered new ways to increase life expectancy, we slowly began the process of outliving our fertility.

Women, in particular, must muddle through this period of middle age called menopause, a time of significant bodily change: drop in hormone production; vaginal dryness; hot flashes; lost of fertility, etc. As an aside: the time period from when perimenopause begins until the onset of menopause can last as long as ten years. In speaking of the physical changes due to perimenopause and beyond, Doctor Nancy Lee Teoff and Kim Wright Wiley state:

"The first changes you're opt to notice are in the outer genitals. Pubic hair thins and the labia loses fat tissue, meaning your vaginal lips become less full and less responsive to touch. Inside, the walls of the vagina thin and become more fragile as a result of the decreased blood supply. If the vagina is not stimulated through sexual play or masturbation, the diminished circulation will eventually affect the nerves and glands.

As the nerves lose function, there is less sensation during intercourse, and as the glands lose function, there is less lubrication. Needless to say, many women at this point are avoiding intercourse, thinking, "Why bother?" But abstinence accelerates the cycle of deterioration. The phrase, "use it or lose it," may sound unsympathetic, but it's accurate." [Nancy Lee Teaff, MD and Kim Wright Wiley, Perimenopause—Preparing for the Change (Rocklin. CA, 1995), p. 158.]

"Unless your moral or religious principles forbid it, masturbate. One contributing cause to dystrophy of the primary and secondary sexual organs is lack of use, and regular masturbation results in improved blood flow to the genitals, cessations and even reversal of poor circulation to the genitals, and some amount of endogenous secretion Of hormones, including oxytocin. As I stated earlier, masturbation is not damaging physically. ... It can be helpful in keeping up your sex organ tone if your frequency of sexual intimacy is not up to your needs." [Paul Pearsall, Ph.D., Sexual Healing (New York, 1994), p. 220]

Once this troubling period of life is over, usually by the early fifties, a woman's sexual life takes on a new dimension.

While women generally can't reproduce after age fifty, they still desire a sexual relationship. Fertility has ceased but sexual desire has not. In fact, a woman's sexual life is often better after menopause than before it. Doctors tell us this is due in part to the fact that many women fear a late age pregnancy and, therefore, shy away from having sex to insure they don't conceive. After conception becomes impossible, a certain sexual liberation and renewal can ensue. In fact, many menopausal women relate that they actually have a stronger interest in, and desire for, sex once pregnancy becomes inconsequential. Indeed, they are more relaxed and focused. With a large measure of anxiety removed from sexual activity, a woman can become free to explore her own body and enjoy the pleasure of carefree sex, especially with her sexual partner.

With regard to men, while they retain a certain degree of fertility their entire lives, they seldom impregnate a woman after age seventy. However, sexual interest and desire still remains present.

One might ask the question, "Does a man or woman ever become too old for sex?" The answer is NO, as long as their sexual organs are in working order and regularly stimulated.

Many doctors believe sexual activity for older folks is therapeutic. One reason for this belief is that sexual activity provides mild exercise, and increases self-confidence and overall mental, emotional, and physical vitality. After the rigors of work and raising a family has subsided or even ended, individuals and couples can enjoy sex even more than in their earlier years. In fact, a significant measure of the isolation and depression which can be part and parcel to older age, can be negated by an active and regular sex life with the right loving partner.

We ought never to identify intercourse solely with reproduction. God gave a woman a limited time frame in which to produce other human life, yet the pleasure and psycho/social dimension of sex obtains from puberty to the grave for both sexes. God did not intend for pleasure to cease simply because fertility is lost.

Dr. David Ruben has stated that, "Sex is one of the two renewable pleasures available to human beings. . . . The other renewable pleasure is eating. . . . Just as there is no valid reason to give up eating at an arbitrary age, there is no reason to give up sex." (Ruben, p. 388.)

So why give it up? It would appear that some people, at least in times gone by, never really felt at ease with sex. This stems from a rigorous religious upbringing. Others just stop engaging in sex after they lose their partner. These individuals want to give up sex voluntarily, or they give sex up because they have no one with which to share themselves. However, many mature adults just lose their sexual desire due to lack of use. Men who were "sexual animals" in their younger years, seem more prone to sexual disinterest as they age. This is partly the result of the inability of older men to perform as well sexually as they did in years gone by. The penis is simply not as lively at sixty-five or seventy years of age as it was in youth.

Many findings have suggested that after age sixty-five, if sexual activity is stopped or even interrupted for long periods of time, sexual capability (especially in men) may not return to a fully potent level, whereby sex can be performed to a person's satisfaction. These periods of sexual "abstinence" can be the result of illness or the loss of a sexual partner due to divorce or death. It would be at this point in a person's sexual life where **M** becomes a recommended option.

"While masturbation is not the ideal form of sexual activity and certainly cannot compete with heterosexual intercourse for lasting satisfaction, it has a significant place in everyone's sexual evolution. Just as masturbation initiates sexual activity in childhood, it can perpetuate sexual function in old age. If the alternative is permanent loss of sexual powers or temporary masturbation, most normal people are likely to opt for a little masturbation. If a husband dies, it is entirely reasonable for a wife to masturbate to keep her copulatory mechanism functioning. . . . Because of the delicate and evanescent nature of the erectile mechanism in older men, it is almost essential for a recent widower to exercise his organic machinery to literally keep it alive." (Ruben, p. 392.) It seems that certain bodily functions need constant reinforcement as we age. Sexual ability is one of these bodily functions.

One question that is often asked by older men is, "Does prostrate surgery inhibit sexual performance?" The answer to this serious question must be qualified. Yes it can, but not in every case. The removal of the prostrate gland is always a medical decision. An obstruction due to a benign or malignant condition which requires its removal does seriously impact on male sexuality. Clearly, the most noticeable change is ejaculation. Once the prostrate is removed, virtually no seminal fluid is released at the point of orgasm. The pleasurable feeling or orgasm can still be present but little or no fluid is ejaculated.

Because a prostrate condition can exist for a long period of time before surgery is performed, many men can experience a period of sexual inadequacy. Due to the fact that an overly enlarged prostrate can interfere with the passage of bodily fluid through the urethra, ejaculation can be somewhat inhibited and urination is somewhat difficult. If the bladder is not permitted to be fully drained upon the urge to urinate, engaging in sexual activity can become a frustration due to the need to urinate during intercourse. And as any man can tell you, the last thing he needs to feel when attempting to copulate is the urge to relieve himself. For the man, a full bladder is an enemy of enjoyable intercourse.

After the prostrate condition is corrected, some men feel more sexually potent than before. This could perhaps be traced to the fact that the urethra is no longer blocked. These men feel better and experience a sense of rejuvenated self-confidence. However, a certain percentage of men experience impotence after prostrate surgery. It serves us well to remember that most prostrate surgery occurs during or after male menopause. (Yes, men do experience a form of menopause.) Many of the cases of impotence associated with prostrate surgery are actually psychologically initiated. This experience can be traced to a loss of sexual self-confidence which is attributable to a combination of male menopause, diminution of the hormone testosterone, absence of ejaculation, and perhaps, "marital fatigue." Men, take heart. There is a sex life after prostrate surgery.

Actually, potency problems in general can be common among both males and females. In fact, the older we get, the more likely we will need some type of medication to treat a chronic illness or medical condition. Some prescribed medication, for example, certain drugs used to treat high blood pressure or depression, can diminish the sex drive or a person's ability to engage in sexual intercourse.

[Note: For comprehensive information regarding the effects of prescription drugs on sexual functioning, see [The Essential Guide to Prescription Drugs (New York, 1995) pp. 1110-1114.]

The male is probably more prone to be adversely affected because the penis is a much more fragile sex organ than the clitoris. If you experience a lack of sexual desire or functioning, see your doctor. If your particular medical problem allows, most doctors will be more than happy to prescribe a different but similar medication. Frequently, there are a number of similar drugs available to treat the same medical condition. Finding the right medication can be tricky at times, but it is worth the hassle.

Another common problem for older adults is hardening of the arteries which reduces blood flow to many, if not all, parts of the body, including the penis and clitoris. In fact, the blood vessels which directly supply blood to the genitals could themselves be the site of a plaque buildup and thus hardening. This condition calls for and requires medical treatment since the danger of blood clots forming is high. A loosened clot in a major artery or blood vessel can cause a heart attack and/or stroke. (By the way, there is a possibility of a stroke to the penis itself.) Any reduction of blood flow, no matter what the cause, can adversely affect the engorgement of blood vessels in the genitals and thus seriously reduce the quality of a man's penal erection and a woman's swelling and clitoral erection. The result is a diminution in one's sexual performance.

But often, the loss of sexual desire and poor sexual functioning can be traced to a low level of the male hormone testosterone. After menopause (male and female), it is common for the body to experience a diminishing of sex hormones. We already know that women experience lower levels of the female hormone estrogen after menopause. However, what many people do not know is that women, like men, obtain a great deal of their sex drive from the male hormone testosterone. Men have in their bodies a large amount of testosterone and a small amount of estrogen. Women have a large amount of estrogen and a small amount of testosterone. Of the two hormones, testosterone plays the larger role in sexual drive and desire.

Replacing low levels of testosterone, that is bringing testosterone levels in the bloodstream back to normal, can do wonders for your sex life. Today, many doctors and researchers recommend a combination of the aforementioned hormones for menopausal women. For men, the newly developed testosterone patch seems to be working out well for those who need to wear it. If you feel that you require something to "jump start" your sex life, contact your physician about this patch.

It is a known fact that testosterone supplements can help restore potency, but the best method to rehabilitate sexual life is to activate the brain. Always remember that the "primary"sexual organ is not the penis or vagina: It is one's own mind. Sometimes, a good romantic novel or provocative video proves to be a potent source for sexual arousal.

One of the reasons the brain is so important to a sexual life is that, while the mind can initiate good sexual activity, it can also be the cause of sexual dysfunction.

Many of the cases regarding impotence occurring in both males and females are not the result of a physical cause. Rather, the cause is mental or emotional. Stress, distress, marital discord, worries over children, fear of disease, fear of not performing well sexually, severe anxiety, guilt, phobias, and the like, all contribute to psychological impotence. These problems need to be treated by trained professionals. Most of the time, just talking to a psychologist, psychiatrist or sex therapist can restore one's confidence, overcome one's fear and uncertainty about the sexual future, and set emotions back on track. (The average medical doctor is a wonderful, competent professional, but generally, he or she is not an adequate counselor when it comes to sexual matters.) It is the brain which will ultimately provide the energy to the penis and clitoris. As I have previously noted, the human brain is our best aphrodisiac.

Sometimes, if one's sexual organ is not reacting positively due to psychological difficulties or disuse, a recommended plan for regular masturbation will be suggested. This may require the assistance of a sexual partner or the use of a mechanical means such as a vibrator. This device can be of great benefit to both men, and especially women, in achieving penile and clitoral erection. Once erections are again achieved on a regular basis, there is no reason why they cannot continue indefinitely, absent other medical problems.

Here are some last thoughts.

Arthritis, as everyone knows, is a condition which causes aches, pain, and swelling in the bodily joints. It is most common among older or elderly people. At times, those suffering from the pain and discomfort of arthritis can reach a point where sexual activity is uncomfortable. Frequently, this condition moves people to curtail or even stop sexual activity. However, if possible, this decision is generally inadvisable. The reason: mild exercise is always helpful to those suffering from arthritis. Sexual activity in any form, but especially when an orgasm results, is a good form of mild exercise. (It has been suggested that sexual arousal and an orgasm release a form of the anti-inflammatory hormone cortisone. Corticosteroid has been used to treat arthritis.) If the arthritic condition is not extremely severe, what more pleasurable way to assist the entire body than a little sexual exercise with a loving partner.

So relax, mature adult sex is here to stay. Just remember that after age sixty to age sixty-five, you have to "use it or you may lose it." All organs, especially sexual organs, atrophy with extended non-use. To keep them vigorous, regular sexual exercise is recommended. This may require you to practice periods of solitary sex: **M**, employed as a transitional activity until a suitable, loving sex partner is found. Masturbation keeps the sexual organs in good working order, provides emotional self-confidence, and helps relieve physical stress. **M** ought to be used as a medical, emotional tool to keep alive the sexual fires, while the goal of reestablishing loving intercourse is pursued.

CHAPTER FOUR

"M": Its Physiology and Technique

Part A - Men and Masturbation

Part B - Women and Masturbation

In this chapter, we will discuss the manner in which men and women masturbate and the various means and methods they use.

PART A - MEN AND MASTURBATION

You may find what I am about to say somewhat puzzling, and understandably so, since I am a man. The truth is, I have found this chapter the most difficult to pen. The task of writing a book is arduous at best, and many a keen mind wrestles with the content and style of a particular section in his or her manuscript. So it is with this section.

My struggle was neither with personal embarrassment nor the reluctance to address a topic that is unmentionable in macho American thinking. Rather, my struggle was to find sufficient material which sheds light upon a delicate, "taboo," issue. Quite simply, given the plethora of information on sexuality, detailed literature on the topic of male masturbation is sorely lacking. A greater volume of information is available relative to female masturbation. Sections on

M in sexuality books, sex manuals and articles in scientific journals abound. However, in all such sources, comprehensive treatment, a telling description, and detailed information regarding male **M** is minimal and fragmented. This problem is not due to a lack of effort by the medical or scientific community, but can be traced to the societal and religious taboos relative to **M**. Hence, there is reluctance on the part of men to cooperate or participate in any medical or scientific studies, sexual research, or behavioral surveys regarding masturbation. The majority of men just refuse to admit that they masturbate.

Of all the researchers in this area, Shere Hite, I believe, has been the most successful in placing before us an extensive body of information obtained directly from anonymous male respondents. (Masters and Johnson and the New Kinsey Study were also good in gathering applicable data.) Nevertheless, we have more than sufficient direct and indirect evidence to draw solid conclusions about male masturbation and offer detailed descriptions of how men masturbate.

Before we examine male sexual stimulation and the techniques of male masturbation, let us present some facts and attitudes that build upon, and somewhat clarify, what has already been mentioned in previous sections.

* Men masturbate more often than women.
* Approximately 80-90% of men masturbate at least occasionally.
* By contrast, approximately 68-85% of women masturbate at

least occasionally.

* For the majority of men, M is a regular part of their sex lives regardless of their marital status. Shere Hite reports that only 1% of men who responded to her study did not masturbate.
* M represents a larger share of a man's sexual outlet while unmarried. It seems a man engages in masturbation far more often when he is without a sexual partner.
* Most men are very secretive about masturbating. Very few are willing to admit "doing it" to anyone.
* While a large number of married men masturbate, and view M as a harmless activity, the majority of both married and unmarried feel masturbation is not "totally justified" within marriage. "If you have an active sexual partner, there is no need to go it alone."
* It seems the majority of men enjoy M physically more than psychologically. Physically, masturbation relieves sexual tension, helps overcome sleeplessness, and feels good especially when lonely.

Psychologically, men find that **M** produces guilt, shame, and a feeling that they lack self-control.

* When men in behavioral studies speak negatively of M, words like depression, loneliness, emptiness and lack of warmth tend to surface.
* Many men believe **M** is fine when you are a boy or teen but not when you are a "man."
* A great number of men feel uneasy after they masturbate even though they thoroughly enjoy solitary stimulation to climax.
* Behavioral studies indicate that most men would prefer to be with someone else sexually rather than masturbate.
* Men, when aroused sexually, are inclined to release the tension (so called, "empty the testicles"). This could be related to the discomfort of vascocongestion which can (but not always) result from strong sexual arousal without ejaculation.

* A large number of men masturbate when the "real thing" is unavailable. Unavailability can be defined as having no sexual partner; a sexual partner who is sick or chronically ill; so called "scheduling problems"; when a wife or lover is having her menstrual period; when one party or another does not desire to engage in frequent sex.
* Men by nature tend to be goal oriented. Sexually, the goal is to achieve orgasm and/or to bring a partner to orgasm. Women are somewhat less orgasm oriented.
* Both males and females find that **M** offers sexual independence. They can engage and enjoy solitary sex and not feel that the subsequent orgasm is dependent upon anyone else. For both sexes, M is convenient and without the psychological pressure to perform well.
* Men tend to feel more at ease with **M** when they feel justified in doing so.

The following are two quotations taken from the Shere Hite report that highlight the male emotional attitude toward masturbation.

"Most men, even though they continue to masturbate regularly throughout their lives, including many times during which they had an otherwise active sex life, felt that they should not masturbate, and that masturbation was basically acceptable for a man only as a substitute for sex with another person---- many adding that they felt defensive, lonely or guilty about doing it." [Shere Hite, The Hite Report on Male Sexuality (New York, 1978), p.487.]

From behavioral research, we have discovered that many men, while engaging in M, find masturbation psychologically uncomfortable. Perhaps this feeling can be traced to the negative social or religious attitude toward sex ingrained throughout history. Possibly, it is instinctual. Whatever the reason, this much is clear: most men masturbate. They do so for pure pleasure or as a substitute for sex with a partner. Most enjoy it physically, but the majority find **M** to be a bit unsettling psychologically.

One of the respondents to Shere Hite's questions stated, "Masturbation is important for me because it keeps me from adultery. My wife would be happy with sex about once a week. There's no way I could survive that without masturbation." (Hite, <u>The Report on Male Sexuality</u>, p. 488.)

Emotionally, all of us desire to share our bodies with someone we love (romantically). Somehow it feels better, and this is how it should be for most human beings. But sometimes, we lack or are denied the physical bonding with another person. At this point, **M** enters the scene for most adults.

Fantasy and Visual Stimuli

The elements which differentiate male masturbation from female masturbation are visual fantasy and stimuli.

It is obviously true that one's imagination is the key to sexual stimulation. The universal opinion of researchers is that the brain is the "ultimate sex organ." A person's mind triggers sexual arousal. However, the mind is stimulated by what one sees and hears. The old philosophical axiom may be operative here: "Nothing is in the mind which is not first in the senses." No matter, we know that the human sexual response is at first cognitive.

Men are visually oriented. They may think sexual thoughts but they seek visual images. While both men and women need to think about sex in order to become sexually aroused, men frequently search for visual images of sex. A man's erotic thoughts conjure up images of girls they have known, women they have seen, sexual acts they desire to experience. Therefore, many males are wont to employ pornographic pictures or x-rated videos to stimulate their minds. Reading sexually explicit material will arouse a male, but not as intensely or quickly as "seeing sex." Hence, many men masturbate while looking at a "dirty" magazine or during the course of viewing a sexual video. Males like to see sex in action performed by others. By contrast, women are prone to mental stimulation via thoughts and words. Many women are more quickly aroused by reading a sexually romantic novel than by viewing a sexy video. These women would rather think sexually than see sexually. Whence, a significant number of women stimulate themselves with mental images. (This does not mean women are not visually stimulated. Clearly, they are.)

As a note of interest: A blurb appeared in The Philadelphia Inquirer on February 11, 1997 under the heading Personal Briefing by Marc Schogol which highlights the vastness of the sex market. He writes: "Looking for a career with a future? Consider the pornography industry. Last year, Americans spent more than $8 billion on hardcore videos, peep shows, live sex acts, adult cable programming, sexual devices, computer porn and sex magazines, according to U.S. News & World Report. That's more than Hollywood's domestic box office receipts and larger than all the revenues from rock and country music recordings."

The notion that men are more visually oriented when it comes to sexual arousal is not a startling revelation. Women have understood this fact for millenniums and have "played up" the visual dimension of sex in order to attract the male, and feel sexually attracted to him. (Men, on the other hand, play up the emotional dimension and love connection to attract women.) Since a man's visual approach to sex is well known, for decades, fashion designers of women's clothing have pandered to this male "weakness" and to a woman's desire to show off her body. This accounts for outfits and clothing which accent a woman's breasts, legs, hips and buttocks: low-cut dresses, miniskirts, the numerous varieties of underwear and nightclothes, various forms of "sexual" lingerie, etc. (We have only to look to the popularity of stores like Victoria's Secret to validate this observation.)

Furthermore, advertisers of almost any product add a sexual twist to their marketing. Whether it is bras and panties, cars or jeans, ice cream to cosmetics, even cigarettes, subtle to provocative sexual images are continuously presented to the public.

Sexual Stimulation in the Male

The question might be asked, "Do men sexually stimulate other parts or areas of the body apart from the penis?" The answer, indeed, is a resounding, "Yes."

We know that the penis is the male's primary sexual organ (apart from the brain). It comprises the glans (tip), the corona, that area of roundness which produces a discernable "head," the underside of the penile shaft close to the tip or head called the frenulum, and the entire shaft itself.

The penile area near the base of the shaft is a good area of stimulation but not great. The further you move up the shaft toward the head, the greater the sexual sensation. In fact, the base of the head on the underside where the skin tends to "bunch up" (frenulum) is the area of greatest sexual feeling for the average male. (We'll note some exceptions later.) The glans or head is oftentimes, like the clitoris in a woman, too sensitive to be continuously subjected to stimulation, and therefore, the entire penile shaft is stroked until orgasm is reached.

This extra sensitivity of the glans introduces us to an unusual twist in the male sexual anatomy: circumcision. While females do not display two different looking sexual organs, men do: the circumcised and uncircumcised penis. The circumcised male has had the skin covering the penis (which is like the hood of skin covering the clitoris) surgically removed at birth. [Circumcision can be done in adulthood but the consensus of medical and psychological experts is that if a boy is not circumcised at birth or immediately thereafter, the procedure should not be done until the male reaches adulthood by his own choice. To do so earlier would result in a negative impact on psycho-sexual development.]

The uncircumcised male has the loose skin covering the penis (foreskin) left in tact. The decision whether to circumcise is obviously left up to the parents, although in some very low weight, premature or otherwise sickly or fragile newborns, the doctor may suggest foregoing circumcision as it could add a bit of extra trauma to a delicate newborn such as pain, loss of blood, infection.

Because the uncircumcised male has a protective sheath of skin covering the glans of the penis, the head of the penis will tend to be more sensitive to the touch. The reason for this is that the head and tip of the penis are not subjected to the friction of being rubbed against clothing, and thus desensitized. With the circumcised male, the head rubs against clothing and body parts making it less sensitive to being touched or rubbed. There are many sexual experts who believe that the uncircumcised have a greater degree of sexual feeling than the circumcised. No one actually knows how extensive the difference is or if it should be preferred.

During masturbation by the uncircumcised male, the sheath of skin is often used by some men to move over the glans or head in a back and forth, up and down motion. Other men pull back the loose skin and expose the shaft and head and stroke the exposed penis until ejaculation occurs. Lubrication is needed by many uncircumcised males in order to avoid irritation of the tender head. (Not every man needs this extra lubrication.) Being uncircumcised does not hamper sexual activity. On the contrary, many believe there is an enhancement of sexual feeling and enjoyment. Being uncircumcised just adds another twist to the mystery of male sexuality.

Regarding sexual stimulation, it may be surprising for some readers to learn that, at times, the majority of men during the act of **M** also stimulate other parts of their bodies such as the anus, and especially the testicles. Frequently, men who are preparing to masturbate fondle their testicles, rub them, move them about and squeeze them. Sometimes, they massage the entire genital area. At times, one hand holds the testicles and the other hand strokes the penis. In addition, some men have reported that they like to hold or squeeze their thighs and legs together.

While male masturbation is generally rather uncomplicated, there are additional actions, thoughts and materials which accompany planned male M. For instance, the male who plans to masturbates usually brings a towel, washcloth, tissues, paper towels or the like to the location where **M** is to occur so as to be equipped to "mop-up" after himself. The male will frequently apply some type of lubricant (e.g., lubricating gel, petroleum jelly, hand cream, saliva, etc.) to the penis to reduce excessive friction and allow the sliding action within the hand or against bedclothes to be smooth. Some men enjoy watching themselves ejaculate by directly focusing on the penis coming or by watching their entire body orgasm in a mirror.

Foreplay

There are a number of men who engage in elaborate foreplay something akin to how women generally arouse themselves: showering, using creams and/or colognes, viewing their nakedness in a mirror, sensual touching of mouth, shoulders, breasts, abdomen, pubic hair, inside thigh area, feather-like touching of the genital area, fondling of the testicles and by placing a finger in the rectum.

As we mentioned, some men like to plan their solitary sexual activity in advance and then prolong the physical pleasure. Once heavily aroused, they start and stop their stroking as they bring the penis and their bodies to the point of a climax. In a sense, as we will see in some women, they tease themselves in order to achieve an intense orgasm. And initially, the stroking or thrusting is short and somewhat casual, but as the building to orgasm increases, so too does the stroking action. Now the strokes become longer and the pace faster. Many men end in a frenzied pace of stroking, gripping the penis hard, and watching the semen squirt out. They then can collapse in sexually fulfilling exhaustion.

Male masturbation is much less complex than female **M**. Men have fewer variations to work with, and ultimately, it is direct penile stimulation which builds pleasure to orgasm.

Types of Male "M"

Although there have been four or five types of male masturbation techniques identified, only two stand out as the overwhelming methods of choice. The other variations taken together represent only a small sample (2-3%) of the male sexual experience. Behaviorally, they are insignificant and the exception to common male **M**. Therefore, we will not examine them in any detail.

The two primary types of **M** employed by males are penile stroking by use of one's hands, and penile thrusting into objects. (Approximately 96-98% of all men who engage in **M** will use one of these two methods to masturbate.) Of these two basic types of masturbation, the stimulation of the penis by one's hands is by far the most common. Most behavioral research indicates that more than 80% of men masturbate in this fashion. That leaves about 16-18% of men who choose to rub their penis against objects or thrust into objects in order to build sexual excitement to orgasm.

These percentages should not be viewed as absolute numbers. In fact, some men who use their hand to bring themselves to orgasm, at times, employ penile thrusting and rubbing against objects.

Likewise, those who primarily rub or thrust their penis into or against objects also use their hands to bring themselves to climax. A combination of different direct stimuli and technique is not an uncommon practice. Women, however, tend to be more exclusive in their masturbatory techniques.

Most men (as do women) masturbate in the manner in which they first discovered how to masturbate. Understandably, in the case of most males, **M** is by hand movement.

> Type I: The stroking of one's penis by use of the hands for the purpose of achieving orgasm.

Masturbation by the use of hand movement is a very simple procedure physically. Once the penis becomes erect, the male wraps his fingers around the shaft and begins to slide the hand over the erected penis until the point of ejaculation occurs and the male seed spurts out of the tip of the penis in three or four jets of warm semen.

This experience can be very quick or prolonged. Many men who masturbate tend to do so quickly as a holdover from the teen years when they needed to have a fast hand in order to "get it over with" before a parent discovered their activity. The drawback to having a fast hand is the development of premature ejaculation when attempting sexual intercourse. Prolongation of penile stimulation is far more satisfying and is a recommended method if future sexual intercourse is to be gratifying for both parties. If a man consistently reaches the point of ejaculation quickly through M, then he will achieve orgasm quickly in the sexual bed, thereby leaving his female partner unfulfilled and frustrated.

Regarding Type I masturbation, the perceived oddity here is that by using the hand to stroke the penis to climax, penile thrusting in general is absent. While it would appear from most studies of male sexuality that the thrusting of the penis is instinctual, the majority of men use hand action, thus bypassing the penile thrusting common to intercourse. As a corollary here, females primarily use finger movement and vaginal insertion as their major instinctual method of **M** which commonly corresponds to coitus. Perhaps in males, the thrusting natural to intercourse is merely transferred to stroking the penis in an up-and-down fashion.

> Type II: The thrusting of the penis into bed cloths or rubbing against an object such as a mattress.

Certain studies indicate that a smaller percentage of males employ this method of masturbation as their usual choice. As with Type I, there will also be times when those who prefer to thrust into objects use their hands to stimulate themselves and even climax. Furthermore, the aforementioned observation in preliminary male stimulation and foreplay also applies to Type II masturbation. Since we have already spoken in detail about foreplay and stimulation, we will forego repeating ourselves. Suffice it to say, that apart from the male "quickie" in the bathroom or shower, most men who masturbate engage in some form of masturbatory foreplay and stimulation.

Logically, one would think that **M** by thrusting the erect penis into an object or rubbing it against something would represent the primary method of choice since it simulates intercourse. But it does not! There is no sound reason for this fact, except to say that the way a male first learns to masturbate is the way he continues to masturbate throughout his life.

But in Type II **M**, we do have simulation of intercourse—a pumping and thrusting of the erect penis into a wad of bed cloths or rubbing the penis while lying on one's stomach and firmly stroking it between the stomach and the mattress using pelvis thrusts.

Some men put a pillow in the bed and place their penis under it and hug another pillow while thrusting as if a woman was actually present. With body weight on the pillow, the penis feels like it is being inserted into a warm vagina especially if a good lubricant is applied to it. (Actually, when practicing this method, lubrication should usually be applied, otherwise, irritation is bound to occur.) Others grasp the penis in their one hand and thrust into the pillow as if it were a woman's mound. Most men who employ this method lie face down on the bed, floor, or couch. Some will lie on their sides and thrust into lubricated hands.

This type of male masturbation is also used by many in sexually restrictive environments since at night, hand movement can be too obvious due to its rhythmic pattern. A certain degree of squirming in bed can be construed as restlessness.

When one thinks of sexually restrictive environments which place the burden of relieving built up sexual tension upon the individual, many examples come to mind. Military bases or naval vessels, boarding schools, seminaries, hospitals and medical facilities, etc., all have sexually restrictive or sexually prohibitive environments.

Individuals in residence at the above noted institutions all experience sexual arousal and pent up sexual tension. Understandably so, for the men in these residences are generally young, sexual partners are absent, and privacy can be at a premium. Some men who live in such places are able to mentally and/or spiritually deal with the temptation to relieve themselves but many are not. Therefore, **M** becomes a release valve, a stop gap measure, which allows the release of sexual tension and vascocongestion. Masturbation under these circumstances becomes a natural physical outlet.

At this point in our study of masturbation, we are somewhat compelled to examine the practice of anal stimulation by males. Anal stimulation is not a third type of male M, but rather, a method of arousal which can intensify the pleasure of orgasm brought about by using either Type I or II.

Shere Hite, in her definitive work on male sexuality, reported that a combined total of approximately 47% of men answering her queries and questionnaires sometimes stimulated the anal area, with about half saying they used interior penetration and the other half external massage or touching.

It was once thought that anal penetration was the choice of homosexuals, and that few heterosexuals engaged therein. Obviously, from Hite's and others' studies, we have discovered this conclusion to be false. Admittedly, some of Hite's respondents were homosexuals, but the percentages clearly indicated that many heterosexuals employ anal stimulation.

The approximately 24% of males who said they used anal penetration did so to create a more intense sexual pleasure. Most, if not all, used one or more fingers to massage the prostrate gland. These men entered the rectum with lubricated fingers and searched the anterior part of the prostrate (a walnut size organ) and massage it.

Some men report intense orgasm can be centered in the prostrate area that is even more fulfilling then penile orgasm alone. Many in this group claim that the climax reached in this way is more intense and that the penile ejaculation is very powerful. However, almost all men reported that they required penile stroking or rubbing in order to put them over the edge. It appears that for the vast majority of men who employed anal penetration, a certain degree of penile fondling is essential. Therefore, some form of hand or body movement of the penis is required to achieve orgasm. Anal penetration alone appears to be insufficient to trigger orgasm in the overwhelming majority of males.

As a curiosity, in addition to the aforementioned methods of stimulation, the following variations have been reported by respondents to major sexual studies:

> (1.) The penis is pushed down between the male legs and pelvic movement rubs the erection to orgasm.
> (2.) Water is used as a primary aid to reach climax: Jacuzzi, water jets, shower massagers, etc.
> (3) Self-fellatio, though rare, does occur. A small number of men appear to be double-jointed, contortionists of sorts,

who can, and do, suck their own penis to orgasm.

Finally, let us just mention in passing that there are some "sex toys" or "tools" which some men employ during masturbation. Some examples are:

(1.) Vibrators - Any one of the various styles of vibrators can be used to stimulate the penis to orgasm. Many men try them. They are particularly good when applied to the underside of the shaft near the head. They are also used by some men to assist them in anal stimulation.

(2.) Dildos - This artificial penis has pretty much one purpose for a male – to penetrate anally and massage the prostrate.

(3.) Inflatable Dolls - This "toy" is an inflatable female doll which has a properly positioned vagina. The male can mount this doll, insert his erection and pump and thrust inside the doll until orgasm is achieved. (It seems like a very lousy substitute for a true woman.)

(4.) "Jerk-off machines" - This "machine" is nothing more than a rubber sleeve similar to a condom which fits over the penis and has an air tube which is attached to a bulbous. As one squeezes the bulb, a vacuum is created so that the rubber sheath grabs the penis, and both squeezes and tugs the erection until orgasm is reached.

To be sure, there are additional "sex toys," for the sexual imagination is fertile. Suffice it to say that the above four give us some idea of tools and "toys" used to bring a male to climax. I do not recommend sex toys. Nature has given us enough avenues of release.

Conclusion

We have taken a glance at male masturbation with its various techniques and "toys." Most men do masturbate, and clearly, marriage is not necessarily a "cure" for **M**. All men find **M** physically pleasurable. But psychologically, they often experience a degree of uneasiness, especially after orgasm. It appears that men believe that they properly belong inside a woman. Masturbation in males as well as females ought to be an interim, stopgap measure employed for release of tension only in the absence of a sexual partner. Getting "hooked" on solitary sex has very little to recommend it.

PART B - WOMEN AND MASTURBATION

I am not certain whether this section will be of more interest to women or to men. Certainly, women will find the varieties of female masturbation curious. Perhaps, some women will be tempted to try a different technique or variation of **M** other than the method they presently employ. Whatever the result, I believe the pages which follow will generally enlighten just about everyone who reads it.

Men who read this chapter ought to pay close attention to the descriptive ways women masturbate. These provide definite clues as to how women are best aroused, and offer a number of suggestions as to how a partner might be better pleasured in the sexual or conjugal bed. Knowing how your partner masturbates is key to understanding her physical needs. Subsequently, we will discuss the direct link between masturbation and orgasm. As we shall see, understanding your body and sharing its secrets, will enable sexual partners to use techniques of arousal which help bring their partner to the peak of pleasure.

To men and women, I say this, "Tell your partner you masturbate and describe in detail the manner in which you do so, and why." Let your partner know how you can best be aroused and led to climax as together you share your bodies and souls in true love making. If you do not masturbate and find sexual intercourse less than gratifying, it is time to try some solitary sex. In this way, you learn about your own needs, and you can communicate to your partner which techniques would provide the proper arousal and ultimate release of pleasure.

When we speak of masturbation, we are really speaking of various forms and techniques of self-stimulation. Even though **M** is circumscribed by a person's anatomy, nevertheless, numerous variations regarding how a person masturbates are in evidence.

Cultural differences, religious prescriptions, societal conditioning, and diverse personal experiences, account for the many methods of **M** used by people the world over. Some people will even go a long way to search for exotic methods by which to pleasure themselves.

Owing to the fact that it is sometimes difficult and awkward to describe how a person builds to orgasm, perhaps it would be useful as a starting point for discussion, to outline in general, the four basic methods of masturbation employed by women. These are as follows:

(1.) Genital stimulation and/or manipulation
(2.) Friction: pressing or thrusting against objects

(3.)   Vaginal entry or insertions
(4.) Thigh pressure or crossing legs while rhythmically pressing thighs together

It should be noted that there are so many variations to the above stated methods that one would virtually go crazy attempting to enumerate all of them. We will offer a few examples and let your mind and imagination fill in the gaps.

Genital Stimulation or Manipulation

Almost every survey, research project, scientific inquiry, study, or experiment indicates that direct genital stimulation is the method of choice for most women. The concept of genital stimulation and manipulation involve a number of different patterns:

(1.) Stimulation of the vulva area
(2.) Stimulation of the clitoral and vulva area
(3.) Stimulation of the clitoral and vulva area plus vaginal entry
(4.) Direct manipulation of the clitoris

As we have learned in the section on male M, women also rely heavily on genital stimulation. The entire vulva area, in particular the labia or "wings" along with the clitoris, are the primary areas of concentration. However, ultimately, it is the clitoris which becomes the object of interest. Since the exposed clitoris is enormously sensitive, most women avoid direct contact with the tip. Rather, women do concentrate their sexual energy on manipulating the area

73

directly around the clitoral shaft. Actually, the entire mons area (the vulva and mound area of the pubic bone) should be stimulated so sexual tension can be built up slowly to prolong sexual excitement, and thus, release a more intense orgasm.

A woman builds to an orgasm in this manner by gentle stroking of the labia, mons and clitoral area, usually with steady movement and slow and increasing pressure applied to that area. The initial stroking becomes more intense and quickens as the building of sexual tension increases. It is this progression which will usually bring the female to the peak of her release. (A gentle tugging of the labia and stimulation of the breasts with the other hand is reported to be helpful.)

During the researching of this manuscript, I discovered two actions which seem to be practiced by the majority of women during masturbation. The first is that approximately 75% of women who masturbate with their hands proceed to orgasm by using a circular motion with pressure applied to the mons, and especially, the clitoral area. The second is that most women (more than 60%) masturbate with their legs spread apart. (The percentages used here and throughout this book are not meant to be scientifically or statistically accurate, since they vary with different researchers. Instead, these statistics serve to assist in drawing reasonable conclusions.) However, the previously described practice represents the primary physical activity used in female M. Some variations apply. For instance, many women draw their legs together as they approach a climax, and utilize up and down hand movements over the clitoral/mons area.

When speaking of manual genital stimulation by women for the purpose of masturbating to orgasm, we can say that essentially this process occurs while lying on one's back or on one's stomach. Shere Hite tells us that lying on one's back is virtually synonymous with the term masturbation.

The most important thing to remember here is not how a woman proceeds to masturbate, but that all masturbatory activity includes strong mental arousal and high levels of concentration. Most women must first get into a state of arousal before any manipulation of the genitals is successful. In sexual activity, physical sex follows and supplements mental sex. Together, they put a woman "over the top."

A small percentage of women masturbate by direct stimulation of the clitoris. Usually, women who employ this method use one hand to tighten or stretch the labia, while using the other hand to touch and manipulate the clitoris directly. Again, mental arousal is key, and unlike with other methods of M, those who directly massage the clitoris, usually settle for one orgasm. The reason for this is sexual sensation when the friction applied encompasses her genitals. This discovery of self-stimulation can be a prelude to regular **M** using friction against objects. When something we do feels good, we tend to repeat the action.

Generally, women use two basic forms of physical activity when masturbating against objects. The first is very similar to the method of lying on the stomach to achieve an orgasm. The essential variant here is that they do not employ the use of their hands to achieve orgasm. Usually, women will "hump" a pillow, rolled up bed sheets, a stuffed animal or some other firm but soft object while lying in a face down position. Women also rotate their hips as they apply pressure on the object, thus stimulating a generalized area in the genitals rather than specifically touching on or near the clitoris. Again, we see the use of circular motion or movements in the pelvic area for the purpose of climaxing.

Many times, instead of lying face down on her bed, a woman will take a soft, firm object of choice such as a pillow or rolled-up towel and ride it as if in the saddle of a horse. This humping allows for additional pressure to be placed on the vulva and clitoris. Sometimes, the pressure and rhythm will be soft and easy, while other times, firm and hard. Fantasizing often accompanies this "riding the horse" technique. So, women thrust, "ride it out," rock to and fro, bounce on the bed, etc. Any pelvic movements which build to climax can be employed.

The second form of stimulation used with this method is the employment of furniture to manipulate and arouse the genitals. A woman who masturbates in this manner might place herself astride the back or arm of a chair and hump it or grind her pelvis on it. Actually, any object that is firm but somewhat cushioned can be employed for the purpose of reaching a climax. It is not the object that is critical here, but the pressure exerted together with the movements of the hips and pelvis which cause a woman to arouse, build sexual tension, and release in a flooding climax.

Of course, in this method of M, as in all others, it is really the stimulation of the clitoris which brings a woman to her peak. Either of these methods simply tugs or presses the clitoris in a somewhat different way, using various bodily positions.

Vaginal Entry or Insertions

In this section, we will be speaking of direct vaginal entry by objects other than one's fingers. While studies have indicated that a much smaller percentage of women masturbate by inserting objects into the vagina, there are those who do, and women have done so for centuries.

Even before the invention of the vibrator, women had discovered that common household items as well as certain fruits and vegetables were conveniently shaped to provide vaginal pleasure through deep penetration. Bottle necks, broomsticks, candles, ceramic items, douche nozzles, plastic objects, bananas, carrots, cucumbers, and sausage are only a few. Only the imagination can limit the number of these makeshift devices. All of the previously mentioned fall under the term dildo. A dildo is basically defined as an artificial penis.

It has been reported by archeologists that the Egyptians were among the first to use dildos. When excavating the tombs of Ancient Egypt, scientists discovered artificial penises fashioned out of clay. The Middle Ages, it has been said, made use of sealing wax to fashion a pleasure rod for a lady. Apparently, **M** goes back a long, long way.

Today, a dildo is usually fashioned out of plastic or rubber, but it can be made from any hard material. In fact, one of the most popular dildos is a gel-like plastic penis that vibrates and feels just like a man's penis.

A contemporary description of a dildo is provided by Dr. David Ruben as follows:

"With the discovery of vulcanization of rubber, the French, who have always displayed ingenuity and verve in sexual matters, developed what is called the underline consolateur. or consoler. Made of virgin gum rubber in the shape of a long, firm but pliable penis, the device was fitted with a reservoir made in the form of a scrotum. This was filled with hot water (some ladies preferred milk) which circulated through the entire apparatus to give the effect of body heat. One model was rigged to spray a jet of warm fluid into the vagina at the psychologically appropriate time." (Ruben, p. 199.)

Following the development of the electric vibrator (especially the battery power variety), most of the old tried and true dildos fell into disuse. Though originally sold as an apparatus to massage the scalp and tone facial muscles, the electric vibrator was quickly adapted for use as a tool to assist in masturbation.

Today, many electric vibrators are designed specifically for sexual purposes, and come in all sizes and shapes, some with different "tips." Generally made of plastic, they are easily washable and very hygienic. The "best" and most "precise" models are made of latex rubber with the shape and feel of a human penis. There are some women who claim that you can't tell the difference except that the artificial one gets the job done better!

Yes, the vibrator represents the ultimate vaginal insertion and many women use it faithfully. It is clean, versatile, and distributes sensation in all the right places. Virtually all insertions are geared to mimic the male shaft in shape and purpose. Some are hygienic while others are not. However, the goal of each type of insertion is to stimulate the clitoris, steadily and rhythmically until that moment of ecstasy arrives, and arrives, and arrives.

Thigh Pressure

We have seen in the foregoing sections that a "golden thread" runs through all the principal forms of female **M**—clitoral stimulation and pressure or muscle tension. This brings us to the discussion of thigh pressure as a means to effect orgasm.

I find this method of female masturbation to be particularly advantageous to its user. The reason being, it is so neat and efficient. The thigh pressure method virtually allows a woman to orgasm anytime, anywhere—in "public" or in private. Since women who masturbate in this manner employ pressure and muscular tension exclusively, a climax can be achieved without the use of one's hands (or other "props") in a sitting, reclining, or even a standing position. Clearly, this technique to achieve orgasm is the most versatile form of female **M**. Curiously, a smaller percentage of women employ this technique, even though it is far more efficient, versatile, and mostly undetectable. In many ways, it represents the ideal method of masturbation for women.

If this method of **M** is so ideally suited to women, then the question arises: "Why don't more women use thigh pressure?" Well, this is a good question with no clear answer. I think the best answer that can be given is that we are all creatures of habit, and since most young females first discover orgasm through fondling of their genitals, they tend to stick with that means of masturbation. Remember, if the way in which we do something feels good to us, we tend to repeat it.

However, since muscular tension and pressure seem to be essential to female orgasm, we know that women who use their hands for clitoral stimulation or thrust into objects, will frequently be employing some vulval tension and pressure during their activity (most often using their hands). Whereas, a woman who uses thigh pressure to arrive at an orgasm rarely employs any other of the masturbatory techniques we have previously discussed. It appears this method tends to be exclusive in its use.

"While a woman who needs to have her legs together to orgasm may have slightly more trouble teaching new lovers ways to have intercourse in which can orgasm, it is also true that women who hold their legs together are more likely to be able to have many sequential orgasms than other women, since they do not stimulate their clitorises so directly (The bunched-up skin forms a protective cushion.) Whatever body type a woman has, she can have fully as much pleasure as every other woman. All she has to do is be active and explore." (Hite, The Hite Report, pp. 204-205.)

Doctors HA. Katchadourian and D.T. Lunde in their definitive treatment of Sexuality entitled, Fundamentals of Human Sexuality (New York, 1972), describe for us the thigh pressure method of **M** on pages 221-222 as follows:

"Thigh pressure is an exclusively female method. When a woman's legs are crossed or pressed together, steady and rhythmic pressure can be applied to the whole genital area. This method combines the advantages of direct stimulation and muscular tension. It can be indulged in practically anywhere the woman may be and can be detected only by the particularly observant."

The doctors go on to quote Havelock Ellis as he provides a description of one such episode:

"....A few years ago, while waiting for a train at a station on the outskirts of a provincial town, I became aware of the presence of a young woman, sitting alone on a seat at a little distance, whom I could observe unnoticed. She was leaning back with legs crossed, swinging the crossed foot vigorously and continuously; This continued for some ten minutes after first observed her; Then the swinging movement reached a climax; she leant still further back, thus bringing the sexual region still more closely on contact with the edge of the bench and straightened and stiffened her body and legs in what appeared to be a momentary spasm; there could be little doubt as to

81

what had taken place." [Havelock Ellis, <u>Studies in the Psychology of Sex</u>. Vol. 1 (New York, 1942), p. 180.]

Havelock Ellis has given us a description of thigh pressure masturbation as executed while seated on public transportation.

Let me now add an incident that I witnessed while attending a major league baseball game. It was a cool September evening, late in the game, and I was a bit "bored." (My team was losing badly.) I left my seat and went down the ramp to the inner corridor of the stadium to have a smoke. Across from the ramp entrance was a small corridor with a rail leading to an exit ramp. In the corner of this corridor by the rail were two teenagers about seventeen or eighteen years old locked in an embrace and kissing with some degree of passion. The young girl was leaning against the rail, her right leg supporting her weight and her left leg crossed tightly over her right leg at the ankles with just the tip of her toes touching the pavement. After a couple of minutes, she raised her left leg and moved her ankle about as if to regain blood circulation and quickly resumed her crossed leg position. In about another minute, I heard a gasp and slight moan and she collapsed in the arms of her male companion for bodily support. A few seconds later, they exited hand in hand. Again, there can be little doubt as to what had occurred: thigh pressure had produced an orgasm while standing in a ballpark stadium.

It is probably true that most women who employ thigh pressure do so while reclining on a sofa, bed, or even on the floor, but the two previous accounts are but two examples of the versatility of this technique: the bed, the train, the stadium, reclining, sitting, standing. Of course, as with all incidents of M, however and wherever they take place, strong mental concentration is a must.

Enough said. Let's take a look at exactly how thigh pressure masturbation works. We will take as our example, **M** as applied while lying down, since most women who use this technique do so in a reclining position.

It is the rubbing and squeezing of the upper thigh which places pressure on the entire area of the genitals: the vulva, the mons, the vagina, and, of course, the clitoris. This creates a generalized area of stimulation, but as the women start to build toward a climax, the pressure and muscular tension begin to localize the feeling in the clitoris. The rubbing and squeezing of the thighs need to be accompanied with steady, rhythmic movement and pressure.

First, a woman lies down either on her back or her side, crossing her legs so that upper thigh pressure can be applied to the genital area. She then begins to squeeze the upper thighs together, pressing tightly, holding the squeeze, then releasing the pressure. This pattern of tense, hold, and release is repeated over and over again, generally more slowly in the beginning, then kicking up the rhythmic pace a notch and systematically increasing the pace until she spills over the edge at the climax.

Some women also choose to place firm but soft objects between their legs before establishing the tense, hold, and release process.

Many find the use of pillows, bed clothing, towels, etc. provides more localized pressure on the clitoris. (Some women also fondle their breasts and place their arms around their head and neck.)

Whatever the variation, it is the tightening, squeezing, tensing, clenching, holding, releasing action that stimulates the genitals, builds sexual tension, raises the sexual sensations to a plateau, and triggers flooding, peaking, sexual release. This pattern is accompanied by mental concentration and oftentimes fantasy.

We can conclude our discussion here by stating that while the thigh pressure technique appears to be very versatile, it is not for everyone. If the pattern of teenage **M** was clitoral stimulation by hand, learning the thigh pressure method will probably take some doing. Likewise, the teen who first discovered recognizable orgasm through thigh pressure, will have a difficult time learning to masturbate by hand stimulation. The principal problem here is learning how to release the orgasm. But remember, if you can orgasm in one way, you can orgasm in another. It just takes practice.

In a subsequent chapter, I will be continuing our discussion of thigh pressure, as I believe this method of masturbation offers the possibility of some surprising results for many women who have trouble reaching an orgasm during intercourse.

CHAPTER FIVE

M To O:
Masturbation: A Tool in Reaching Orgasm During Intercourse

The foregoing chapter has provided us with an overview of how people masturbate and the many different ways and means employed to achieve this end. Now let us turn our attention to the use of one's masturbatory techniques for the purpose of aiding a woman in the achievement of orgasm during sexual intercourse.

What has become quite clear over many decades of research is that the physical and emotional elements involved in the act of masturbation are more complicated and complex when engaged in by a woman. Therefore, it is altogether logical that if orgasm during intercourse is a problem for couples, the party having the more difficult time climaxing will be the woman. Hence, this chapter will be devoted almost entirely to a woman's use of **M** to assist her in achieving orgasm with her mate.

There have been more than sufficient studies, interviews, and research to indicate that many women have difficulty reaching orgasm during sexual intercourse. As a matter of fact, it is fairly safe to say that between 40% and 50% of adult women having sexual intercourse fail to reach orgasm by coitus alone. However, this fact does not, in any way, let the male off the hook when it comes to the responsibility he shares for enjoyable, satisfying intercourse. He must be a willing and cooperative partner in this wonderful venture. If he is unwilling to do what is required and necessary to help his partner build to her peak during intercourse, he has failed in his responsibility as a loving mate to assist in establishing a satisfying and fulfilling sexual union. If he would persist in his uncooperativeness, the relationship is pretty much doomed. Quality sex is essential to the cementing of a union between average healthy people. Failure to do all that is required to provide for quality sexual satisfaction is to assure the relationship's demise.

Various sciences discovered long ago that the failure of a woman to attain an orgasm cannot be attributed willy nilly to female inadequacies. Indeed, in most instances, the male fails to properly arouse and bring the female slowly along through adequate foreplay and emotional bonding, which would prepare her to build sexual tension and reach her peak of release. In addition to inadequate foreplay, the male, at times, reaches the point of ejaculation before his female partner reaches her orgasmic peak. Once spent, the male simply relaxes and retires, leaving the female, highly frustrated. If you read on a regular basis, any of the "women's magazines," you will quickly conclude that there are a great many women sexually frustrated with themselves and their partners.

Different bodies; different minds

The irony here is that many of the frustrated sexual encounters are not the direct fault of either party. Rather, the quirks of human nature enter the picture, and force us to adjust our behavior. For instance, some women can reach a climax quickly, while others need a much longer time frame. On the other hand, some men can thrust within a woman dozens of times before they reach the peak of satisfaction. Other men need only thrust ten to twelve times to explode in an orgasm. You see, John Gray is correct, "<u>Men Are from Mars, Women Are from Venus.</u>" Our bodies are different—our thought patterns are different—our needs are different. Is it any wonder that sexual frustration creeps into the bedroom?

A woman who is generally not sexually satisfied by her loving partner is frustrated and feels somewhat inadequate. A man who usually ejaculates prematurely feels, at times, less a man, namely, that he is not able to properly satisfy his loving lady. In any event, sex impacts either positively or negatively upon a relationship.

Marriage discord

More marital trouble can be traced to the bedroom (and all the other emotional baggage we bring along into the boudoir) than to any other single factor in marital discord. Most marital hostilities will sooner or later surface in the bedroom. Money and employment, or more specifically, the lack thereof, represent two additional and very important issues in any marriage. But, these are cognitive and factual problems. Sexual frustration is an emotional and physical problem, and hate-filled emotion is what will ultimately ruin a relationship.

To quiet my critics here—sex per se is not the sole or even the main cause of marital failure. Rather, it is in the bedroom that the trouble usually surfaces. Please understand. I am in no way oversimplifying the cause of marital disharmony and divorce. I am merely stating, very simply, that an inadequate sexual relationship is always lurking somewhere near the center of tensions. Sometimes, sex is *THE* cause, often, it is a symptom of *THE* cause. It has been my experience that when a couple works vigorously at mutually satisfying each other's physical and emotional needs, particularly in the bedroom, a significant degree of frustration is jettisoned from the relationship. Thus, feeling sexually at one with the other, together they can address the additional issues which constitute living together.

Working toward mutual satisfaction: know your body

Masturbation can become a simple but effective tool to be used in establishing good satisfying orgasms during intercourse. Engaging in **M** within the context of intercourse is not to be viewed as a good, in and of itself. On the contrary, **M** in this situation is for teaching and training sexual partners to reach mutual sexual climaxes.

(Note: I am not referring here to "coming together" or simultaneous orgasm. This is an experience seldom achieved during intercourse, even by the best of minds and bodies. What I am referring to is that each person reach orgasm sometime during the sexual encounter.)

By the way, it is always preferable for the woman to orgasm prior to the man. This allows her to experience complete sexual pleasure, and then turn her attention to the man, allowing him, without fear of "counting strokes," to enter her inner chamber and share his manhood. Moreover, by employing masturbation as an instrument to train the body to orgasm, we remove **M** from the realm of private, solitary sex and move it into the framework of shared sex which is what nature intended sex to be: a mutual coupling of body and soul.

The examples of masturbation that have been heretofore demonstrated provide us with certain clues as to how to achieve orgasm during love making. Perhaps by taking our cue from the various techniques previously outlined, we can adjust our bodies and minds to apply "our own method" (or try another) to further the sexual fulfillment desired and richly deserved. Barry McCarthy, in his book entitled <u>What You Still Don't Know About Male Sexuality</u> (Toronto, 1977), pages 21-23 respectively, offers us a few well-chosen thoughts regarding the importance of knowing your own body and its sexual responses when it comes to sexual sharing. He writes:

> "Seldom do we give ourselves the chance to realize that masturbation, far from being a shameful necessity, is actually one of the best possible ways of learning about our sexual responses and of increasing our sensitivity to sexual stimulation—lessons that can then be applied with enormous profit to partner sex."
> "Masturbation need not be only a way of triggering

brief, intense sensations localized in the penis. It can be a method of awaking the sexual potential of the entire body. As such, it can serve to vastly increase a man's capacity for sexual response with a partner."

"....Our heightened self-awareness will make us more conscious of our partner's sexual needs and responses. .. . Thus, in the sense that a 'real man' is one who is knowledgeable about and responsible for his own sexuality, who can respond and interact sensitively with a partner, masturbation can serve to enhance your masculinity."

These observations apply equally well to both male and female.

A woman who has difficulty climaxing with her partner can practice masturbation and apply this experience to drive her toward reaching orgasm during sexual intercourse. Some women may require the use of a vibrator to arouse themselves to a climax. The goal here is to practice achieving a climax by the use of a mechanical means and, once so conditioned, transfer this experience to sexual intercourse. One word of caution is necessary: since the more we masturbate, the more we desire to do it, **M** can become an easy habit of solitary sex, rather than the intended segue into satisfying intercourse. Careful attention as to why we are practicing **M** will help keep us on track and maintain our focus on utilizing masturbation as a means to reaching our physical, emotional and spiritual goals.

A taste for sexual gratification which masturbation provides, can, and should, lead a person to seek total sexual pleasure with another person. The objective here is to harness and direct the use of **M**, so as to furnish the missing link for couples whose sexual relationship is somewhat disappointing (at least to one party). There is no facile or absolute answer to any couple's sexual frustration. Indeed, there exist enough sexual manuals to fill a room which are dedicated to the proposition that couples need to be taught proper sexual techniques. While these books serve a good purpose, most are similar in content, and if they had the answer to sexual fulfillment, they would rid the world of much discord and turmoil. But alas, no magic solution has been found. What we do know is that knowledge of our bodies via solitary sexual activity often leads to the ability to carry on a mutually satisfying sexual experience. **M** is but a tool. It doesn't offer complete answers. Rather, masturbation merely directs us to use self-knowledge in order to bring about satisfaction in any sexual encounter.

> ". . . . Masturbation increases your ability to orgasm in general, and also your ability to orgasm during intercourse. Why not? It's the same stimulation. Only 19 percent of the women in this study, who did not masturbate, orgasmed regularly from intercourse—quite a drop from the 30 percent in the overall population. Of course, masturbating to orgasm does not automatically enable you to orgasm during intercourse. There is no mythical connection between the two—just the practical experiences with orgasm—how it feels and how to get it." [ShereHite, The Hite Report (New York, 1977), p. 202.]

Shere Hite begins her subsection on "the connection between orgasm during intercourse and masturbation" with the above statement. You will see clearly during this presentation that **M** has a rightful place within the confines of learning to orgasm during intercourse.

Since most women are brought to an orgasm by stimulation of the clitoris-intercourse imitates masturbation. Yet most women still have trouble experiencing an orgasm brought on by a man's penis. Research suggests that in the act of M, the feeling is more direct and intense so most women can climax fairly easily by solitary clitoral stimulation. A man's penis does not provide the same pinpoint stimulation, hence, it can become difficult to reach female orgasm during intercourse relying upon penile stroking alone.

Shere Hite, speaking to women has this to say:

> "We do give ourselves orgasm, even in a sense, when something else is providing us with stimulation, since we must make sure it is on target by moving or offering suggestions, and by tensing our bodies and getting into whatever position(s) we need —and then this is a final step necessary in most cases: We need to focus on the sensation and concentrate, actively desire, and work toward orgasm." (Hite, The Hite Report, p. 206.)

It seems that while male and female bodies are well suited to copulation, it is not so well designed for stimulation. Extra effort by both paries is required for proper stimulation to occur. Since women have the overall problem of achieving a climax with their loving partner, they need to take a long look at how best to apply the knowledge of their own body to discover how they might have intercourse and come away satisfied. Certainly, understanding their own experiences with **M** is critical to achieve mutual satisfaction in bed. "To have an orgasm during intercourse . . . first and most important, she must consciously try to apply her masturbation technique to intercourse or experiment to find out what else may work for her to get clitoral stimulation." (Hite, The Hite Report, p. 200.)

A woman must employ a great degree of concentration to help her maintain a complete focus upon what is occurring within her body and take responsibility to help stimulate herself so as to be in a position to climax with a man. A male has the onus of extending every effort to help his female partner arrive at her peak of pleasure. He must provide the additional physical stimulation she requires, and through gentleness, soft-spoken words, and tender touches, evoke the emotional atmosphere needed for complete fulfillment of sexual lovemaking.

Women must begin to take charge of a sexual encounter because men may not be as sensitive or understanding of a woman's need to be brought along to orgasm.

Women today must study their own bodily reaction to sexual stimuli, and then do what is necessary to maximize their sexual sensations so as to insure the arrival of orgasm. The following statements are some reassuring comments made by women to Shere Hite as quoted in her monumental report on female sexuality:

(1) "Yes, you can't just lie there and wait for an orgasm. You sense that one is approaching, and so of course you concentrate on helping it."

(2) "At a certain point you have to stop relaxing and having fun and build yourself up to this earthmoving experience. . . ."

(3) 'For many years, I was unable to have orgasm with another person; Then finally I taught myself to tense my body so much that I'd push myself over the brink."

(4) "The concentration of your mind must be focused with all your might between your legs—on the vagina."

(5) "I had to learn to make an effort, not lie back and wait for "Jove's Thunderbolt."

(6) "You have to learn to move your body to get maximum stimulation for orgasm."

(7) "Yes, a woman often has to learn how to achieve orgasms in spite of her partner, not because of him." (Hite, The Hite Report, pp. 206-209.)

These women are telling Shere Hite (and all of us) that to experience gratifying sex with a man, a woman must take charge, direct the man's sexual activity, and ultimately, do what is needed to bring on her climax. Obviously, concentration by the female is a key element in reaching orgasm, but the fundamental route taken to arrive at orgasm is masturbation. Since masturbation is "learned" in solitude and practiced in quiet privacy, the concentration so key to climaxing is relatively easy because there are no distractions. But there are distractions in the sexual or conjugal bed: another person. Therefore, total concentration is not as easy to attain. Translating the experience of **M** to sexual lovemaking with one's partner will, at length, become crucial to arriving at the point of ultimate release during intercourse. A middle-aged woman recounted the following:

> "I am thirty-eight, married and have two children. I had intercourse for the first time with my husband when I was twenty-seven years old, three years before we were married. He was and is the only person I've slept with. About three months ago, I had my first orgasm, except for a few in the past two years during sex dreams. I really wanted that first orgasm, worked at it, and rejoiced when it happened—during masturbation. Now I have orgasms all the time and I love it; they get better and better. I masturbate at least two times a day, usually more, and always have orgasms. It took longer to learn to have them during intercourse, which happens with us every two or three days, but now I always do. . . ." (Hite, The Hite Report, p. 135.)

The following is a brief summary of what Shere Hite concluded from her extensive research on female sexuality regarding orgasm during intercourse.

> "The women who had orgasm during intercourse were usually those women who, in a sense, did it themselves. They did not expect to 'receive' orgasm automatically from the thrusting of the partner."
> "The cardinal rule is you must make it happen yourself, not just wait for it to "happen," or for him to happen to hit the right spot out of luck."
> "The most successful women have adapted their masturbatory techniques unabashedly and unashamedly to relations with others—or else have just been unusually lucky in having a very sensitive and knowledgeable partner." (Hite, The Hite Report.

p. 201.)

The foregoing statements obviously tell us that mastering the "art of masturbation" is, perhaps, the essential ingredient required for most women to climax during intercourse with her partner or husband. One of the reasons so many women in the past have experienced such disappointing sex with their partners is that they have failed to master the methods and techniques of **M** unique to them, and carry their personal "expertise" over to the act of intercourse. Of course, we already can surmise why this was so. Religious and secular society heaped too much guilt upon the masturbator. To practice techniques of **M** was anathema! Therefore, many women masturbated reluctantly and without a conscious effort to master bringing on orgasms which could be used later as a tool to establish satisfying lovemaking with their spouse or partner.

While the times have changed, many of the ingrained attitudes toward masturbation have not. Yet, we do see in much of today's literature on sexual activity and sexual matters, advice relating to the use of masturbation as a helpful transition from solitary sex to mutual fulfillment.

John Gray, in his book <u>Mars & Venus in the Bedroom</u> (New York, 1995), pages 102-103, talks about a situation where the husband is disinterested in "doing it," while his wife was longing for sex. The husband tells his wife, "Why don't you go upstairs and start, and I'll join you later.". . . . "When he got into bed, Sue was already prepared for an orgasm because she had spent the last forty-five minutes becoming more and more aroused, fantasizing about David making love to her while she caressed herself. It was no wonder that after about two minutes of penetration she had an orgasm. After seconds later, he had his." He continues, "She made the best of the situation . . . Taking a long time to touch herself in a sensual way and masturbate herself, she slowly built up her sexual tension so that when he entered her, she was already about to have an orgasm."

In the above account, John Gray tellingly places before us an example of how masturbation can become a very useful tool in aiding couples to arrive at mutual sexual satisfaction, as they give themselves over to each other in love. [Also see: Betty Dodson, Ph.D. Sex for One: The Joy of Self-Loving New York: Crown Trade Paperbacks, 1966, and Lonie G. Barbach. For Yourself: The Fulfillment of Female Sexuality New York: Signet, 1975.]

If a woman takes between fifteen and twenty minutes to stimulate herself before she makes love to her man, she goes a long way toward insuring herself a wonderful orgasm and, in addition, uplifts her partner who senses that he was a significant contributor to her ultimate pleasure.

Here's another suggestion. Since a man can become aroused in a matter of seconds, and, even when awakened from sleep, can quickly respond sexually, why not take the initiative. Relax, fantasize, touch your body, stroke yourself until you are at the brink of orgasm. Then gently awaken your man, and as he erects, slide him inside you, and in a couple of minutes, both of you will be shuddering in pleasure. It might be a quickie but your peak and his satisfaction are worth the wait. In both of these instances, preliminary self-stimulation via one's masturbatory technique has assisted the couples in arriving at a mutual blending of body, mind, heart and spirit.

All this might sound a lot like one is arranging for a sexual episode. To a great extent, that is exactly what we are suggesting. No one ever said that planned sex can't be fun. As a matter of fact, most of the time it is better to prepare and plan for your sexual pleasure. Such preparation serves to heighten the moment of spontaneous sex, while at the same time assuring that regular sex is fulfilling even when spontaneity is absent.

Now, let us address yet another question which arises frequently between sexual partners: "What happens when one party is in the mood and the other party isn't?" Even in the best of relationships, there will be many occasions when one lover desires intercourse and the other doesn't. We are all human beings, and we are not always ready or able to perform mutual activity just because our partner suggests it. At least in the sexual realm, this doesn't need to become a problem. Allowing a partner to feel free to masturbate will go a long way in alleviating sexual frustration and intense resentment. If each person feels the other has given them permission to pleasure themselves, then those times when one lover is "horny" while the other is not, will fail to turn into a battle royal. Rather, the party masturbating will release their sexual tension and both will feel comfortable to try again tomorrow. **M** can be a great aid to a marriage or intimate relationship as long as both parties know it is taking place. (Secret masturbation within a marriage is not recommended.)

Spanning a period of fifteen to twenty years, John Gray and Shere Hite offer opinions and cite research that masturbation can be both an effective tool and useful sexual release within a marriage or otherwise committed union. John Gray suggests that couples should always be honest and open with each other. Regarding a woman who is sexually "up" for intercourse while at the same time her husband or partner is not, Gray offers this advice: Try saying to your partner, "I have been feeling really turned on today, and I can see that you are really tired. It's OK if you don't want to have sex, but I thought I would masturbate thinking about you. As I get closer to having an orgasm, if you want to join in at any time, that will be fine with me. If you don't feel like it, that's <u>OK</u> too." (Gray, p. 104.)

Gray further states, "It is very important that a man support a woman's need to masturbate so that she doesn't ever feel deprived of having an orgasm if her body happens to be wanting one when he is not in the mood." (Gray, p. 113.)

We all know that men are usually in the mood. However, more and more studies by today's researchers indicate that stress on the job and in the family have begun to take its toll on men. At times, they, like many women, are "too-tired" to be bothered. But men are easily aroused even when tired, and what frequently occurs is that the man tends to get aroused thinking about his partner masturbating and joins in to climax in an act of intercourse. The very thought of **M** by one can lead to arousal and climax for two. The corollary here is for a woman to understand and appreciate a man's need to engage in frequent sex or experience frequent sexual release. A mutual agreement regarding sexual release can establish a bond of mutual understanding and can further cement an already solid relationship.

Ponder the words of a male respondent in Shere Hite's Report on Male Sexuality:

> "I masturbate at least several times a week—generally each night when I don't have sex with my wife. She knows this, and we've often discussed the matter and she came to understand and approve of it. It has had a very beneficial effect on my marriage because I desire and need sex much more often than my wife, so my being able to masturbate with her approval and understanding, it eventually eliminates the pressure that I would otherwise exert on her to satisfy me. It means that I don't have to be nearly as disappointed if we don't have sex together on a particular night, and my wife doesn't have to feel that she has to have sex with me or I'll be frustrated."
> (Hite, The Hite Report on Male Sexuality, p. 493.)

Clearly, from the above account, we can recognize **M** as an effective tool when used to enhance the sexual relationship. This is true whether the exercise of private masturbation is translated into a fulfilling orgasm during intercourse, or whether solitary **M** is employed with full knowledge by both parties as a sexual release when one party to the relationship is simply not up to having sex.

But as we conclude this chapter, let us return to our original premise: that knowledge of our bodies, gained through **M** allows us to make love to our partner in a manner which is mutually rewarding.

The techniques of masturbation by women may vary but the need to build to climax with a partner does not. One reason that **M** is considered by so many women as a most effective and proficient means to achieve orgasm is that, in masturbation, a woman has absolute control over her body. When another person enters the sexual bed, the unfettered manner in which she climaxes during **M** is inhibited. The freedom to do whatever she wants with her legs, arms, hands, etc. is diminished by another body lying beside her or on top of her. Therefore, a woman must adjust and direct her man to position himself in such a way as to allow for the maximum sexual use of her body.

Curiously, for many women, the thrusting of the erect penis is a distraction. The in and out movement tends to negatively effect the women's ability to fully concentrate. A thumping, humping partner can interfere with orgasm as the point of release approaches. A good number of women seem to enjoy slow, gentle thrusting—not the proverbial penile "battering ram."

Most of the evidence gathered on female sexuality indicates that when it comes to making love, women prefer a steady rhythm they can count on, a rhythm which they can use to help focus their concentration on building to their peak. For many women, the reliability and predictability of a man's penile movement, especially the pressure exerted, is most important in reaching an intense orgasm.

In conclusion: how a woman masturbates will lead her to search out the best means to achieve her goal of physically, emotionally and spiritually rewarding sex. Some women will discover that the stimulation of the clitoris, so vital in M, is best achieved by mounting the man and, once on top, controlling the degree of thrusting, the amount of pressure, the needed rhythm, and the depth of penetration. Other women will find that a combination of extended manual foreplay and full concentration will be all that is required to reach the desired result of a flooding orgasm.

Each one of you must experiment. You need to find the proper and best way for you, individually, to arrive at total sexual fulfillment. For those of you who have trouble orgasming during intercourse, yet have a willing-to-help partner, I offer a proficient method of achieving orgasm during love making if both parties are willing to concentrate and work at climbing the sexual mountain.

The method I will be suggesting in the next chapter allows a woman to use the knowledge of her body to build and reach her point of release, and, at the same time, permits the man to be inside her gently thrusting. The woman will experience a climax and the man will feel that he is the reason she has achieved orgasm.

You see, masturbation, that simple almost addictive experience of youth, once harnessed, can play a vital role in lovemaking and, in particular, can aid in the establishment of a successful marriage.

CHAPTER SIX

A Suggestion For Men and Women

There is perhaps no greater frustration than the inability to reach orgasm when the desire, the time, the place, and the partner seem just right. Such frustration can be experienced by both male and female, but the male almost always achieves ejaculation during sexual intercourse, the female does not. Approximately 40% to 50% of all females who engage in sexual intercourse never achieve an orgasm through penile penetration and stimulation. These women either end their sexual encounter unfulfilled, or secretly masturbate as their partner falls off to sleep. For centuries, many women have probably asked themselves, "Isn't there a better way?" It occurred to me that there is, and I would like to share it with you. Recall that the failure to reach orgasm during intercourse centers mostly around the lack of proper sexual stimulation provided by the man together with a lack of the needed level of emotion and concentration by the female. But also, the way one masturbates has a good deal to do with the frustration. Women know, and men must come to understand, that the female experience of sexual arousal and climax is a far more complex exercise than orgasm for a male. Therefore, we must work together to achieve mutually gratifying results. However, even with extended foreplay, fantasy, and concentration coupled with a patient loving partner, there will be many women who still cannot find the key to pushing themselves over the edge. The fault does not lie with them. Often, the human body is just too complicated. The type of stimuli which help build to orgasm in many women simply does not produce the same results for others. There is no logical biological, psychological, or medical reason for this anomaly. Clitoral stimulation is essential but some women only respond to pressure applied to their clitoris as their stimulus. There is one method or technique in sexual intercourse which just might provide an answer for those women who may require clitoral pressure in order to achieve an orgasm during coitus.

We spoke of thigh pressure as one method for women to attain orgasm through M, let us now return to thigh pressure and see if its versatility can be a key answer to solving a problem many women have: experiencing orgasm during intercourse.

A Suggestion for Men and Women

Couples should begin by getting comfortable and placing themselves in a sexual frame of mind. Always let your minds arouse and lead you. Your body's sexual reaction will soon follow until both mind and body are in lockstep.

Allowing your mind to do the sexual heavy work will keep your body and its sexual parts in good stead and at the ready.

Once you and your partner are together and the mood is right, the softness of your bodies can be felt, the gentleness of your lips and touch experienced, the probing of secret areas achieved, the vaginal juices flowing, the slight dripping of a firm and ready penis, the time is ripe for that wonderful feeling of mutual coupling.

Women, it is at this point that you gently and quietly roll over onto your side near the edge of the bed, placing one leg across the other, while letting the crossed leg dangle over the bed's edge. This allows greater pressure to be applied to the genital area. Your partner then takes to his side nuzzling closely to you. You are lying against one another. Each of you is ready to couple with the other, deeply yet quietly. Just lie there a few minutes and let each other feel and sense the beauty of being one with the other lover. Let your brain go into high gear— leading you with erotic thoughts as you begin to concentrate deeply on what is about to happen.

For women, the process of tense, hold, and release begins. You will squeeze your thighs (tensing them), hold the tension a few seconds, and then release the tension. Your goal is to establish a rhythmic pattern. Repeat this process over and over again as you build. At the same time, men, thrust your penis. As you feel your partner tense, gently push your shaft deep into her vagina, hold it in this position a few seconds and withdraw slightly as she releases her thigh muscle. The woman tenses again while her male partner thrusts—both hold—she releases and he withdraws slightly.

A pattern is now formed. Continue to repeat the process over and over again. A man's shaft does not need to move more than an inch or two within the vagina. He is pressed deeply inside and simply moves his penis forward when the woman tenses. As she builds toward a climax, the rhythm and pace of the tense-hold-release will increase.

At any time during your act of love, I recommend that the man, with his free hand, gently fondle the woman's breasts. Perhaps he can place his saliva on a couple of fingers and gently rub and "pick at" the nipple itself. This can dramatically increase the woman's sexual sensations because, unlike some other method of intercourse, all her sexual areas are at work.

As we mentioned before, it is always best if the man can hold off his orgasm until the woman achieves hers. In this way, the firmness of the penis is maintained throughout the tense-hold-release pattern. Once her orgasm has occurred, he can stop his movements and together, they can enjoy the vaginal contractions which occur when a woman experiences orgasm. (Occasionally, the vaginal contractions will be so strong that they will literally "milk" an erect penis to ejaculation.)

As the woman feels and senses the subsiding of her climax (resolution phase), she can begin again, if she chooses, to immediately initiate the tense-hold-release pattern. In short order, the woman can and will achieve a second, or even a third or fourth orgasm.

Once a woman's body and mind are sexually satisfied, the attention turns to him. He can choose to stay behind her and begin thrusting, or choose any number of different positions such as having her mount atop him, and ride him to climax.

In the end, both of you are sexually satisfied, fulfilled, quenched. A gentle, yet fiery orgasm has been experienced. You, the woman, have attained with your lover, the goal of love: complete emotional and physical fulfillment. *Absent* is the frustration. *Present* is the physical and spiritual dimension of true sex.

Is this method of orgasm easy to achieve? No! This is especially true for women accustomed to using fingers or thrusting for vaginal stimulation. But like all great accomplishments, practice is required, and even variations are necessary. What is so exciting about implementing this technique is that once mastered, the woman will regularly reach a climax and the man will feel that he and his "sexual equipment" played a large role in bringing his lover to an orgasm. Rightly so, since he has indeed led his lover to her peak.

Ponder the result of this technique: Both of you enjoy physical pleasure, both of you experience emotional pleasure. Womanhood is ratified and the masculine need to bring a woman to a climax is satisfied. It's a great combination.

Just a Note

Let me assure you of one thing: this technique used to attain orgasm during intercourse should not be misconstrued as mutual masturbation, but rather, a true act of loving intercourse using knowledge of the body, a pressure technique which leads to orgasm, and a loving partnership whereby each party is not "given" sex by the other. Rather, in unison, both parties, working together as a team, reach their goal.

In addition, let me say that while I urge the use of this method, I do want to suggest that this method or technique is the best, or better then any other, in achieving mutually satisfying intercourse. We are all unique individuals and every marital or sexual union is a unique experience. However, my recommendation of this particular method is founded upon the belief that while no specific technique is the best for everyone, once mastered, the above described suggestion for intercourse is very reliable and has many advantages to recommend it. At length, the best technique is what satisfies and works best for you.

CHAPTER SEVEN

Is "M" Ever Preferable to Other Sexual Activity?

The above question may seem out of place given the overall philosophy of this book—that masturbation, apart from teen years, ought to be used as a tool to aid in orgasm during intercourse, or a substitute sexual outlet: (1.) To keep the sex organ working during a person's golden years; (2.) As an interim sexual outlet when one is lacking a sexual partner or when the sexual partner is unavailable.

So, Is **M** ever preferable to intercourse?

As an end unto itself, masturbation is probably *not* preferable. But there are particular groups of persons with special circumstances whose situation argues to the use of masturbation in place of heterosexual or homosexual activity. Basically, three major categories surface in which **M** is a preferred sexual activity to the alternatives:

(1) Those with the HIV/AIDS virus
(2) Teenagers
(3) Prison inmates

[Note: There are other situations or cases when **M** would be preferable. We will touch upon two of them at the end of this chapter]

Let us reiterate. Solitary sex is rarely as fulfilling, at least emotionally or psychologically, as sharing one's body with another person. Yes, the physical rush is virtually identical, but the overall feeling relative to a person's emotional well-being is absent. To share one's body with another is always more fulfilling than "sharing" it with oneself. "If the final goal of sex were simply orgasm, the ideal form of sexuality would be masturbation. It is cheaper, cleaner, and saves lots of time. It lacks one important ingredient—emotional involvement with another human being. Sex without emotional feeling soon becomes sex without physical feeling." (Ruben, p. 157.)

Those with the HIV/AIDS Virus

Since the discovery and onset of AIDS, masturbation has, or will become, the sexual outlet of choice among those diagnosed with HIV or full-blown AIDS.

The AIDS virus makes casual sex far more dangerous and, indeed deadly, for this and future generations. Therefore, in today's world, **M** looks to many as a reasonable alternative to the terrifying possibility of contracting this dreaded disease. **M** is safe, clean and pleasurable.

The AIDS virus is the greatest scourge ever visited upon this planet. It kills, and does so almost systematically, not randomly. (While the sexual activity involved in its transmittal is frequently random, the manner in which it kills is not.) Systematically, because it involves the transferal of bodily fluids, specifically blood and semen. Therefore, since sex plays one of the major and perhaps ultimate roles in the transmittal of HIV/AIDS, this disease becomes the most insidious of all illnesses because it involves one of the basic functions and drives of human life— sex—the desire to reproduce. (While reproduction is not at issue in homosexual activity, the primal drive to reproduce is what fuels all sexual activity, even sexual actions which can never result in conceiving another human life.) People neither can shutoff nor shut down a basic human drive. They can only channel it: in the case of AIDS, into a safer sexual experience.

Enter the **M** Word!

While we have said that **M** is best used by adults as a tool to help achieve a fulfilling heterosexual relationship, AIDS forces us into a limited rethinking of this position. If ever there was an argument for the primary use of M, AIDS has provided the "final reason."

AIDS is still a *very* misunderstood disease. In fact, most Americans still have no idea of the many facets of this illness. It is not just some disease one contracts, experiences pain and discomfort from, and then quickly succumbs to in death. On the contrary, traveling the road from the initial diagnosis of being HIV positive, to the onset and experiencing of full-blown AIDS, to death, can take many years. During these years, those who are HIV positive do not jettison their sex drives, and therefore, their sex lives. These unfortunate individuals must struggle to find a sexual outlet. Some continue to have "protected sex" with a partner or lover.

Their lover or partner may likewise be HIV positive, but often they are not. When the lover or partner is not HIV positive using a condom is not an absolutely safe course of action. We all know condoms break. When HIV or AIDS is not present, the breaking of a condom, at worst, signals the possibility of pregnancy or the contraction of one of a number of the other sexually transmitted diseases. But if the condom breaks during sexual intercourse when one of the parties is infected with HIV/AIDS, the results for either partner can be disastrous. Remember, if a man is not HIV, the exposure of his penis through a ruptured condom can allow a woman who is HIV positive or has AIDS to infect him, especially if he has lesions on his penis or a urethral infection. We already know if a man is infected, the depositing of semen in a woman's vagina through a ruptured condom will usually transmit the infectious virus, especially if there are any cuts or tears in the vagina. (Anal intercourse practiced by most homosexuals and many heterosexuals is particularly dangerous since the likelihood of blood and semen mixing is very high, and the chance of a condom rupturing is dramatically increased.)

Question: Is it completely safe to have sexual relations with someone who is HIV positive or has AIDS if they use a condom?
Answer: NO!
Question: Are persons who are HIV positive or have full-blown AIDS relegated to having solitary sex?
Answer: NO!

With their partner, they can enjoy the physical and emotional pleasures of mutual masturbation. This is safe sex, and is strongly recommended under these circumstances.

(Note: Regarding intercourse, a condom still remains the safest alternative apart from abstinence.)

The question might be asked, "If both partners are already infected with HIV/AIDS, why bother with a condom or practice abstinence?" The answer to this question is simple, medical science appears to have identified different strains of the HIV virus. One strain could be more virulent than another. Two persons with HIV could have unprotected sex, and as a result, one could transmit the more virulent strain to the other. (The more virulent strain will probably be less responsive to drug therapy.)

Another factor to consider is the manner in which AIDS causes death. Due to the fact that AIDS effects the destruction of a person's immune system, other infections or diseases apart from the AIDS virus are allowed to enter and attack the body. At length, these illnesses cannot be combated by a person's immune system even with the help of drugs. The AIDS virus doesn't kill you. It allows other viruses, bacterium, etc. to cause death.

It might even be possible for a penis or vagina to harbor bacteria, which once introduced into the body, results in a disease leading to death. (Note: Presently there is no strong evidence of this occurring.) By the way, oral sex is likewise very dangerous (even with a condom) and ought to be avoided. If semen enters the mouth through unprotected oral sex, and any lesions or open mouth sores are present, the probability of contracting HIV/AIDS rises dramatically.

The only safe sex for HIV/AIDS sufferers is masturbation, either individual or mutual.

In conclusion, sex between two HIV/AIDS infected individuals can be dangerous but it doesn't mean that these individuals who suffer from this disease cannot have a fulfilling sex life. Couples infected with HIV/AIDS should consult the various sex manuals to familiarize themselves with the wide range of sexual activity which does not involve intercourse or oral sex. Those infected should use sexual stimulation techniques in the same manner as those not infected. Their sexual sharing ought to include kissing, (Kissing is only dangerous if bleeding gums or open mouth sores are present), touching, 'Foreplay." Orgasm may still be the goal, but it is the means of achieving a climax which makes for a truly fulfilling sexual experience. Once the sexual fires are red hot, orgasm can be brought on through mutual masturbation. **M** is truly the only safe sex.

To HIV/AIDS sufferers, I say, keep the fires burning—keep your sexual desires alive—but channel them so as to share your bodies in a safe manner. Employ the physical and emotional experiences of the past to share the warmth of human coupling in the present.

Teenagers

The statistics are frightening: A majority of teens have experienced sexual intercourse by their nineteenth birthday. This is a sad trend and bodes poorly for the future of our society. While teens may by all appearances possess a man's or woman's body, they lack the emotional development to handle the complexities of sexual intercourse. Quite frankly, teenagers can copulate, but the true meaning of intercourse is lost to them. They do not view having sex as the ultimate act of human sharing, the act wherein God's gift of supreme physical pleasure unites with a person's heart and soul. Teens are simply unable to appreciate, deep within their entire psyche that sexual intercourse is where heaven and earth unite.

If we require any proof of the irresponsibility of teenagers relative to sex, we need only look to the number of teen pregnancies in America. I will not bore you with statistics. They are too sad to recount anyway. But the numbers point to a horrendous problem— sexual immaturity and complete ignorance of the true consequences of intercourse. Ponder for a moment the tragic cases of teenage girls cleverly hiding their pregnancies, delivering full term babies, and then killing the newborns to avoid detection and the responsibilities which attend to the birth of another human being. Assisted at times by their boyfriends, these young people not only block out the ramifications of conception, but go so far as to deny to themselves that their actions are homicidal. Not only can a pregnancy result in the destruction of a human life and a teenager's future, certain individuals are emotionally crippled for the rest of their lives.

Sex is not simply physical. It carries a tremendous emotional impact, especially in young women. Teens simply do not digest the fact that sex is one of the most complicated and complex human acts.

Today's world encourages and tolerates all forms of sexual activity. But the sexual liberation of America in the 1960's and 1970's was meant to be an adult revolution. Children were supposed to be protected. What happened?

Television, Hollywood movies, cable programming, the print media, advertising companies, and even computers carried sex to new levels. (The birth of the Internet has caused a monumental problem.) These media outlets portrayed sex as a widespread, thoroughgoing, casual experience that everyone ought to taste. The media and computer industries did not expose the beauty of sex nor did they raise sex to a higher level of physical and emotional sharing. Rather, they have lowered the spirituality of sex by treating it casually, shallowly and with banality. Media moguls have yet to understand that physical sex should always be portrayed within a meaningful and loving context.

All this sexual casualness filtered down to children and teens, "teaching them," if you will, that sex is a game. It's fun. It feels good. Sex surely feels good, to be sure, but it's not a game. Sex is one of the most important and significant experiences of human life.

As a result of the irresponsibility of the media and corresponding adult behavior, teens witness sex portrayed in a trivialized manner. Society exposed teens over the last twenty-five years to an "age of sexual license." Unfortunately, they are ill equipped to handle the mental and emotional intricacies of sex. Teens have become the unwitting victims of the sexual revolution.

We must begin to establish better and more efficient supervision of teenagers.

Parents or guardians have to close off some of the opportunities provided for teens to sleep together. A special NIGHT LINE "Town Meeting" addressed the subject of teen sex. Ted Kopel spoke directly to teenagers. The fact that most of the teens present admitted that they engaged in sex should come as no surprise, but where and when sexual intercourse took place most often, might: in their own homes, in their own beds! These teens even openly discussed the opportune time for engaging in sex—between 3:00 P.M. and 5:00 P.M.— from after school until before their parents come home from work.

Kopel mentioned that when he was a kid, even if you wanted to have sex, there was no place to do it. Most kids didn't have cars, and there was always somebody at home—your mother, a grandparent, or a sibling who couldn't be trusted. When the opportunity is denied, the action is foregone.

Well, I am afraid that the latchkey kid is here to stay. Therefore, education will have to suffice as a means of reducing dangerous sexual activity. Since teens pay very little heed to the consequences of their actions, parents and educators face a monumental task with regard to sex education and reasonable moral behavior. Kids today are more academically and socially advanced than their counterparts in previous generations, but as all educators and psychologists know, academic ability does not necessarily translate into, or always correspond to, emotional maturity. In fact, we are witnessing more and more, the commission of horrendous crimes by teens with a privileged upbringing

One example of teen immaturity is glaringly evident regarding the distribution of condoms. Many, if not most teens, just throw them away. And, it isn't because they don't intend to have sex. There is a high school bus stop near my home. I pass by this place many times. Do you know what I regularly see lining the gutter and curb at the point of drop off?—dozens of new, unopened packs of condoms. Enough said!

Something in society must change to assist teenagers in seeing sex in a proper light, with a proper perspective, in a proper meaningful context. This task of educating youth to sexual meaningfulness is herculean because sexual activity has gotten out of hand with teens. In the meantime, we must understand that "teen hormones" will not allow teenagers to keep their sexual drives in check. Therefore, masturbation must somehow become *the sexual outlet.* This approach will require that we tolerate **M** as normal adolescent behavior and allow this activity to occur without ridicule or scolding. Masturbation ought not to be taught per se, but tolerated quietly.

Should adults and educators encourage and promote masturbatory activity among teenagers? No. However, it is incumbent upon us to understand that **M** is preferable to copulation.

Hopefully, as teenagers mature into well rounded young adults, they will graduate from "playing with themselves" to safely sharing their body's physical, spiritual, and emotional power with another human being. However, until such time, we must understand that masturbation, in whatever form (individual or mutual) is to be preferred to intercourse.

Prison Inmates

Let us just briefly consider the problem that incarceration presents to both males and females in terms of sexuality and sexual drives. (Note: The word *intercourse* when used in this particular section refers principally to anal entry.) Just because persons find themselves in prison doesn't mean that their hormones stop surging or their genitals cease functioning. On the contrary, the lack of opportunity to engage in sexual activity can lead to heightened sexual desire owing to the absence of an outlet.

Since the penal system (at least in the U.S.) completely segregates males from females (Each sex has its own penal institution.), heterosexual activity is virtually nonexistent. But this doesn't preclude that sexual activity is suppressed or diminished. In most prisons, sexual activity is a regular occurrence, but owing to the nature of the system, sexual encounters between inmates are relegated to the arena of homosexual activity.

Many inmates are forced by fellow inmates and even prison guards to perform homosexual acts. The younger the inmate, the more likely he or she will be a target for the "seasoned inmate." Some engage in homosexual activity in order to become a sexual partner to a "prison gang leader," thus allowing this individual to be somewhat "protected." Others make "friends" and use each other as an outlet for their sexual energy. Being forced to have sex is one thing. It can't be avoided. <u>Choosing</u> to have sex with another inmate can, and should be, avoided for physical, mental and emotional reasons.

Homosexual activity in prison is prevalent and widespread. But most occurrences relative to homosexual behavior are not truly free choices. Certainly, coercion is not, and even inmates who reluctantly "choose a partner," do so for mere expediency, and not because they are true homophiles. A naturally restrictive sexual environment calls for the only reasonable and safe sexual outlet—M.

Every human being, including prison inmates, will become sexually aroused from time to time, and some on a regular basis, and will need to relieve themselves Due to the fact that **M** represents a clean, effective release for sexual tension, masturbation is to be preferred to the alternatives while one serves out his or her sentence.

In conclusion, there may indeed be other reasons, times, circumstances and situations which would call for **M** as opposed to homosexual or heterosexual activity. But, quite frankly, I can't find any which fall into a major category such as the above mentioned, and also fit into the scope of this book. However, before we end our discussion, I feel compelled to note two possible exceptions:

  (A) Masturbation by and among those persons who surfer
      from mental or emotional retardation and those with
      developmental disabilities.
  (B) Masturbation by those who have taken vows of
      celibacy and/or chastity

Let me say at the outset that I am not about to tackle these two issues in depth. It would serve no useful purpose here. The reasons ought be quite clear:

(1) These topics are far too complex, complicated, and convoluted to devote anything less than a book length manuscript in order to give this issue of **M** in these contexts the weighty presentation it deserves and demands.
(2) The above issues are far too controversial. The emotions inevitably evoked would only serve to cloud the truth and distort facts.

The above being said, may I add that while masturbation by and among the mentally and developmentally disabled and those individuals who have taken vows of celibacy and chastity falls within the context of the question "Is **M** ever preferable?", it does not fall within the parameters of this book. Nevertheless, I will offer some remarks and observations on the subject of **M** by the mentally deficient and celibates.

Just because an individual lacks reasonable mental capacity or suffers from some form of developmental disability does not mean that they are sexually neutral. Although these individuals may be mentally underdeveloped or dysfunctional, such individuals are *not* sexually impaired. As this group of persons reaches puberty, hormonal changes have the same effect upon them as on their healthy counterparts. Their minds may be impaired, but once they experience sexual pleasure, there exists a strong desire to repeat the good feeling. The long and short of it is, the mentally disadvantaged masturbate. Owing to the fact that this group of people cannot (in general) meaningfully engage in heterosexual intercourse as we understand it, or appreciate the spiritual and moral essence of this act, **M** is definitely the preferred sexual activity. (Note: The above topic is so complex that sexual experts and counselors cannot completely agree on how to sexually educate the mentally and developmentally impaired. If you are interested in reading more on this "tough topic," a thorough and excellent presentation can be found in Rosalyn Monat-Haller's Understanding and Expressing Sexuality.

While it is questionable whether celibacy should fall within the boundaries of this book, it definitely does not fit into this discussion: Is **M** ever preferable to intercourse or homosexual behavior? The answer is fundamental. Those who take vows of celibacy or chastity have by their promise excluded all sexual alternatives: **M** cannot be preferable, because in theory, there is nothing to be preferable to. (Yes, some individuals violate the dictates of their vows by engaging in heterosexual or homosexual behavior, but these constitute the exception. And, exceptions to the rule cannot be seriously considered as a topic.)

Of course, reason dictates that even a sincere vow of celibacy or chastity cannot overcome the sexual tension and desire which well up in men and women from time to time. It ought to be understood that **M** by celibates as with **M** by all human beings is a perfectly normal, natural, morally neutral activity. It is only the vow taken which adds a restraint. Therefore, any sensible person understands that even celibates masturbate occasionally, and yes, for celibates, **M** is preferred to giving in to any other sexual temptation.

To recapitulate: many persons find themselves in situations where their sexual drives cannot be reasonably or legitimately socialized. For these individuals, masturbation is the only recommended, or even sane, sexual outlet. While **M** is not the ideal form of sexual behavior, it is a tenable outlet for sexual energy and, at times, must be viewed as preferable to the performance of alternative sexual acts.

CHAPTER EIGHT

Masturbation: Some Pitfalls and Drawbacks

You will recall from the introductory chapter that we noted that there exists no evidence whatsoever to support any claim which would suggest that masturbation produces ill-effects to a person's body, mind or soul. Quite simply, **M** is not physically nor psychologically harmful in and of itself.

Like most activities of human life, there are pros and cons for M. We have already stated that masturbation is principally a morally neutral action. But this is not to say that masturbation is to be recommended, nor should we construe that the activity is best avoided. Rather, there will be times in one's life when **M** is unavoidable; when **M** is recommended; when **M** is helpful; when **M** is preferable; when **M** can be detrimental.

In any instance, there can be drawbacks to masturbation, pitfalls which can lead a person to employ masturbation for the wrong reasons. These drawbacks are not bad or wrong in and of themselves, but may lead to feelings of guilt. Or, the act of masturbation may become so habitual and easy that a person begins to prefer it to intercourse. Additionally, **M** can, for some individuals, produce a negative impact upon a sexual relationship. "Masturbation viewed within the framework of psychoanalytic theory, is thus a universal and normal activity of childhood and adolescence and a legitimate adult activity when coitus is not possible. It is considered harmful, however, when it engenders guilt and anxiety—and symptomatic of sexual immaturity when it is preferred heterosexual intercourse." (Katchadourian and Lunde, p. 232.)

We would be remiss to cite the benefits of masturbation without, at least briefly, pointing out some of its drawbacks as well.

Guilt

Many men and women have said that they experience tremendous guilt and uneasiness after they masturbate. These feelings of guilt should come as no surprise to us, since it has been drummed into our heads for centuries that masturbation is a wrong, evil, despicable act which produces all sorts of terrible physical and mental disabilities: from pimples to the loss of hair; from the growth of hair on the palms of men's hands to the inability of a wife to satisfy her husband; from blindness to heart disease to insanity etc., etc., etc. All forms of horrendous scourges would be visited upon those who masturbated.

Of course, all of this pious drivel is false, and has been debunked by science for many decades. Yet, the residual effects regarding warnings of personal plague and the moral admonitions of clergymen are with us still. "Untold number of persons have suffered mental turmoil from childhood onward because of guilt about masturbation. It is probably fair to say to that never have so many been so indebted to so little for so much anguish and guilt. Clearly, such upset is due not to the act of masturbation itself but to the entirely unnecessary feeling that one is bad, worthless, perverted or sick . . . Thus any adverse effects of masturbation are attributable not to the masturbation itself but to mistaken notions about it." [Warren R. Johnson, Ph.D., Sex Education and Counseling of Special Groups (Springfield, Illinois, 1975) pp. 88-89.]

At this point, I would like to mention another reason why masturbation could elicit guilt feelings. To a minor degree, guilt feelings, anxiety, or uneasiness about masturbation might possibly stem from Natural Law itself. Namely, that since sexual intercourse is an instinctual drive in all animal life, any use of the sex organ which eliminates or bypasses intercourse may naturally produce a bit of guilt in humans. However, it is strong, severe, and debilitating guilt which concerns us, for it represents a pitfall of **M** that can adversely affect one's life.

Some people find themselves caught up in a pattern of **M** which causes strong feelings of guilt, encourages the loss of self-esteem, and robs them of self-confidence. Perhaps more is at work within these individuals than guilt about the act of masturbation. Masturbation, here, could be merely a symptom of underlying emotional or psychological problems. (We do not know this for certain. Only a competent psychiatrist will be able to determine on an individual basis whether underlying problems exist.)

Solitary sex has always carried a degree of guilt for all people. This is why it is performed alone, in solitude. Rarely, do individuals feel free to say to their sexual partner, "I am going to the bedroom to masturbate." Virtually no one even thinks about telling anyone, even in this sexually liberated age, that they intend to masturbate, or that they even masturbate at all. The act of **M** remains to this day, a socially unacceptable and somewhat guilt-ridden activity.

Masturbation and Marriage

(Solitary sex in any sexual partnership may be detrimental. I have chosen here to single out the marital partnership because the overall consequences of divorce far exceed the pain of just "breaking-up"—palimony not withstanding.)

Candid and frank discussion between sexual partners is absolutely crucial to preserving a marriage or other loving union. This premise can account for the suggestion that a partner should always tell the other when he or she plans to masturbate, and then invite their partner to assist, watch, and join in. This mutual sharing brings solitary sex out of the realm of clandestine activity into the arena of openness.

John Gray, in his book <u>Mars and Venus in the Bedroom</u>, speaks to the subject of **M** as an aid to achieving an orgasm during intercourse but warns: "I strongly recommend that couples should let each other know when they are masturbating, so the partner can at least have the opportunity to join in." (Gray, p. 104.)

Generally speaking, sex is a binding agent for most successful marriages. The sharing of one's body is a sign and symbol of the sharing of souls. If love is present, when a woman opens her legs to her partner, she is actually opening her heart to him. When a man inserts his penis into a waiting vagina, what is actually doing is placing his heart within her. It is for this reason that **M** must be used sparingly within marriage. Of course, **M** is useful as a tool to assist in experiencing fulfilling intercourse. But used alone, outside the deep sharing of love, masturbation can become an obstacle to the mutual blending of lives.

Dr. Warren R. Johnson offers the following thoughts on masturbation and marriage in his book, Sex Education and Counseling of Special Groups: "These days young men and women who have been exposed to reasonably good sex education take it for granted that their mates very probably masturbated while growing up and are likely to continue doing so from time to time in the best of marriages. Still, however, marriage counseling is still sometimes needed to help couples realize that such behavior is not somehow 'bad,' cheating on the mate or a perversion." (Johnson, pp. 92-93.) However, Dr. Johnson continues with a warning: "It would be a mistake to assume from the foregoing that masturbation is necessarily healthy behavior. As pointed out earlier, it may represent compensatory behavior and signal the need for help. In marriage too, it may signal a problem requiring careful evaluation for its meaning, perhaps pathological meaning." (Johnson, p. 93.) (The doctor is speaking here about how **M** can signal a breakdown in communication, internal hostilities, unusual sexual attitudes, or psychological problems.

Clearly, that while **M** can be an aid to the sexual relationship within marriage, it can likewise become a villain. Here are two common examples of how simple masturbation, devoid of any psychological underpinnings, can begin to harm a marital relationship.

Female: A woman feels sexually excited during an afternoon. She showers, uses her favorite body lotion and slips into bed. She fantasizes and touches herself tenderly. After some gentle fondling and more rapid and excited stroking, she reaches her peak and climaxes with a fulfilling moan. Out of breath, satiated with pleasure, she drifts off to sleep.

She awakens refreshed and begins to go about her household chores. After a time, her husband arrives home. She's been in his thoughts all day. They greet, kiss, and he retires to their bedroom, disrobes and showers. Refreshed and renewed, he suggests that they make love. She balks at his suggestion and offers excuses. (You'll recall that she's already sexually pleasured herself unbeknownst to him.) He backs off, remains sexually frustrated, and they wait for another time.

(To a similar degree, the man can sexually stimulate himself to orgasm unbeknownst to his female partner, and, so too, balk at her advances resulting in her sexual frustration.)

Male: It is late in the evening, and a man's female partner retires to their bedroom after casually hinting to her lover that she is "in the mood." He responds, telling her that he has rented a video, and that he will come to bed when the film is over. The movie he has selected is rated X. He pours himself a beer, sits back, and proceeds to watch this titillating show. Before long, he is experiencing an insistent erection, and begins to fondle himself. The more he kneads his testicle and gently strokes his penis, the quicker the sexual pleasure intensifies. In no time, he finds himself in a quasi-frenzied drive to orgasm. The strokes quicken and his grasp becomes firmer. Within seconds, he ejaculates with thundering pleasure. After "cleaning up," he returns to bed. At this point, his wife awakens and begins to make loving advances. He simply doesn't respond to her initiative. She gently continues until he informs her that he is too tired. She rolls over in frustration and awaits a "better" time.

In both of the preceding examples, the partners are wrong. Masturbation was not used to strengthen the marriage bond but rather to weaken it. Solitary sex has replaced marital sex. If this pattern of personal pleasuring continues to recur, the frustration within their marriage will mount and their relationship will suffer.

Both men and women, at times, have a great temptation to privately pleasure themselves. However, for a woman, the natural temptation to masturbate can be more compelling because so often her experience of intercourse is a dissatisfying one. Far too often, a man has a "quick hand and a fast gun." (Almost all women prefer a partner with a slow hand and an easy touch.) The natural temptation to masturbate for a man can usually be traced to the desire to have sexual relations more frequently than circumstances might allow.

Couples have to be watchful not to let **M** (apart from their spouse) become habitual within their marriage. This type of sexual behavior represents a marital pitfall which can seriously injure the relationship. People should take care not to fall into this trap.

Occasional **M**, performed privately within the context of marriage, presents no serious problem and may even encourage the desire to seek the height of sexual pleasure coupled with one's lover. But regular use of masturbation to reach a climax without a concerted effort to jointly come to orgasm or to help, encourage, and teach each other to achieve mutual release is at length, a short road to marital chaos.

As I have said repeatedly throughout the pages of this book, few marriages which possess a strong, loving, sexual relationship, experience "deadly" discord. Every marriage will encounter relational difficulties, to be sure, but the mutual blending of bodies and souls will help see them through. If their bodies and souls are unconnected, marital trouble is just around the corner.

Misuse of a Vibrator

Next, let us examine another great means to enhance the act of masturbation: the use of a vibrator. While helpful to most, the use of this device can be a drawback to certain personalities.

Many women prefer to use a vibrator as a tool to assist them in masturbating instead of relying solely on hand movements, pelvic thrusts, or thigh pressure to achieve orgasm. Those that do so, generally swear by it stating, "It gives me the quickest, most intense orgasm I have ever had."

To be sure, vibrators produce gentle to intense sensations throughout the vulva and vaginal area. These wonderfully localized feelings tend to bring on full blown climaxes in women who regularly use this device to masturbate. Since most vibrators resemble an erect penis in some fashion, these devices encourage the onset of a sexual climax when stimulation is actually resulting from a man's penis.

The key words here are "regular use." If by regular use, we mean a couple of times a week or less, then the vibrator is a good tool to aid in achieving an orgasm. However, if the vibrator is overused on a daily basis or in a habitual manner, it becomes a crutch upon which a woman must rely to achieve a climax. Some women may use a vibrator very frequently and still peak with their partner, but these are the exception.

Therefore, the vibrator as a tool is fine. As a crutch, it is not so fine. Some authors have suggested, that a woman's body may become physically and (more probably) psychologically addicted to its use. Since the intense vibrations and sensations produced by this device cannot be duplicated by a man's thrusting penis, a woman may become so physically adjusted and responsive to the vibrator's ability to engender an orgasm, that she no longer reacts positively to penile stimulation.

I do not mean to suggest that a vibrator is "dangerous" to employ or shouldn't be utilized. On the contrary, it is a wonderful tool to assist women in learning how to orgasm with their partner (if they have difficulty doing so). And, a vibrator has rescued many relationships from unbearable frustration. Quite simply, what we are saying is that a woman relying too heavily upon a vibrator (especially when masturbating) may cause her to "need" it, and if her partner senses this, his self-image, self-confidence, and self-esteem might be seriously wounded. ("I can't pleasure her but a machine can.")

So here's the caution: Don't get "married" to a vibrator. It is a *pitfall* of masturbation which must be avoided.

Excessive Use of Masturbation

No one has to be told that masturbation is habit-forming. We need only to recall our adolescent years for any proof that **M** easily becomes a habitual exercise. But thankfully, most men and women outgrow the *habit* of masturbating as they begin to socialize their sexual activity with a partner.

The question arises: What happens if one doesn't outgrow the constant need for solitary sex? We realize that **M** can remain a habit for some well into adulthood. However, excessive masturbation signals trouble. Of course, no one has yet been able to come up with a definition of the word, excessive, when applied to the context of masturbation. I suppose it is somewhat like trying to define pornography. Most experts have not been able to come up with a solid, uncontroversial definition of "porn." As someone once said some years ago, "I can't define pornography, but I know it when I see it." The trouble is, unlike pornography, we don't see people masturbating. So, it will be principally up to an individual to determine if **M** is becoming excessive. However, we can offer some guidelines to help determine if masturbatory activity is excessive:

> (1.) When a person consistently masturbates three or four times a day;
> (2.) When **M** is practiced regularly or preferred to the detriment of a solid sexual union with another person.
> (3.) When **M** is exercised to the exclusion of another person when a willing partner is available.

If the above apply, something is decidedly wrong with this person's sexual life. Psychological help is called for to uncover the reason for this pattern of solitary sex.

While the above paragraph points to masturbation, which may require some professional attention, note well that normal, healthy, well-adjusted persons can also fall into the trap of masturbating far too frequently than pleasure itself dictates. For instance, if a married person masturbates with greater frequency than they engage in sexual intercourse, their masturbatory activity will disrupt an otherwise healthy sexual relationship. This is a behavioral *drawback* for which everyone should be on the lookout.

There is one test you can employ to tell whether your solitary sex represents a problem. If you ever begin to experience a feeling deep within your mind and heart that your drive to masturbate is taking control of you instead of you controlling it, the time has arrived to curtail masturbation by using willpower or seeking appropriate counseling.

There are many sex manuals today which include a section dealing with masturbation in which the practice is encouraged whenever a person feels the desire or need. I believe this to be a misguided philosophy. For while these books offer this advice in good faith, masturbation should generally remain a substitute activity when a loving sexual partner is unavailable. I do not suggest here that these writers offer or encourage **M** as a replacement for intercourse with a loving partner. They do not! However, if by encouraging self-pleasure, masturbation becomes an end in itself, the goal of mutually sharing body and soul is diminished, and so too, society.

EPILOGUE

Some of you, after reading this book, will find the facts and opinions presented herein hard to swallow. This is perfectly understandable given the religious and social condemnation of masturbation throughout history, and the experience of this denunciation in your personal lives. I personally understand and appreciate how difficult it can be for anyone who has been indoctrinated by organized religion and social convention to believe that masturbation is not a frightening and dreadful activity. (Even though, I suspect, your own mind tells you that it is not so evil.)

Many who have read this book will have been amazed to discover that **M** can, in fact, be a healer of wounds, a helper in overcoming dysfunction, and a sexual activity to be preferred in certain human contexts. While there may exist to some degree, drawbacks and pitfalls relative to masturbation, in the overall, **M** is a morally neutral expression of sexual energy. I am quite certain that many readers were equally surprised to discover that **M** can, at times, be physically, psychologically, ethically, socially, and even medically recommended as a tool to help achieve physical, spiritual and emotional wholeness. That secular and religious societies, despite all evidence to the contrary, cannot see their way clear to accept masturbation as a normal, natural, instinctual form of human behavior, is appalling. What is so inscrutable and hypocritical here is that everyone throughout history who has ever condemned masturbation has very probably masturbated, and in the majority of cases, was enjoying masturbation even as they denounced its use as a sexual outlet. Why people felt such an overwhelming need to attack **M**, vexes me. I can neither understand this to my satisfaction nor explain it to yours. But what I do know is that masturbation might just be the most misunderstood activity in all of human history.

Today, in our modern "age of enlightenment," we need to apply our broad knowledge of human sexuality to masturbation. By studying masturbation within the context of human nature, we can better understand where solitary sex fits into the overall pattern of human sexual behavior. A more thorough look at **M** gives all of us a glimpse at the unifying nature of sexuality. Sex is a common drive and experience which, when used and viewed properly, can become a unifying agent for the forces of love. This is what the sacred marital union is all about—the blending of sex and love with a view to enhancing the higher power within us. When parties to a marriage view sex and love as separate elements, they sentence their union to "death row."

Even outside the institution of marriage, in permanent, committed heterosexual and homosexual unions, sex, love, and fidelity must always hold a center stage. Both inside and outside marriage, the body and mind must become one solitary unit which leads the couple down the road to permanency. Far too long have we separated sex and love. The expression of love is, indeed, the greatest contribution humans have made to civilization. In many contexts, love can and must serve alone. The love of parent for child, the love of brother and sister, the love of intimate friendship, all witness to the higher dimensions of the heart.

But when we speak of marriage and other committed heterosexual/ homosexual unions, we refer to loving relationships which intrinsically involve the physical sharing of ones body. For these unions, sex and love are inseparable. The fact is that, apart from a physical accident of nature, the sharing of bodies is indispensable to the nurturing of this love. Both are required— the body *and* the spirit. The result of the linking of body and spirit is a special union of hearts which cannot be replicated. Together, two persons become one and lead each other into eternity.

The question arises: Where does masturbation fit into this scenario of personal love? The value of masturbation is directly related to its usefulness as a tool to enable people to enhance these loving relationships or as a stopgap measure to relieve sexual stress, or provide a means to keep sexual organs in good order until a loving partner can be found. Furthermore, **M** may be required if one's partner is temporarily or permanently impotent. Masturbation is not an end unto itself, but a means to keep a person focused upon higher goals. Sexually frustrated people do not contribute kindness, patience, and love to a community or society. Rather, the sexually frustrated can be bitter, cynical, and even mean-spirited. Masturbation, while not a "cure-all," can at least reduce sexual frustration and thus enable good people, without a sexual outlet, to let the true goodness of their personality comes forward.

We are not saying that sex is "the" central ingredient of life. But since we are all sexual beings, orgasms play an intrinsic role in the lives of most human beings. At times, these orgasms will be the result of loving intercourse. At other times, they will be self-initiated. Either way, sexual release in some manner is vital to the living out of a human life for all but a very small minority.

Some may quickly question the need for sexual release. Well, nature itself attempts to assist us by providing nocturnal "wet dreams" to both men and women. This unconscious relief of sexual tension is nature's way of keeping humans sexually on track. When conscious, we must deal with sexual interest, urges, and arousal in a different manner.

To direct our sexual energy to another person as an object of love is the general or usual way for people to express themselves sexually. We have seen that even with a loving partner, **M** can be a very effective tool to keep the bodies and minds of couples growing in the expression of love. But absent a sexual partner, **M** can be a temporary method of releasing sexual energy.

Yet, many arresting questions still remain. For instance, what about those members of society who find themselves in sexually restrictive environments? I have purposely avoided addressing the topic of sexually restrictive environments because of the great complexity and controversy which attends such a subject. I will offer a few, brief comments only to "round-out" the topic in question.

A definition of a sexually restrictive living environment might be the following: a place when interpersonal sexual liaisons are prohibited. Some examples include hospitals, mental health facilities, prisons, seminaries, convents, military barracks, etc. (Of course, any intimate sexual activity or overt masturbation is always out of order in public places.) However, all inhabitants of such institutions retain their innate sex drive and their natural need to release sexual energy or relieve sexual tension. Obviously, masturbation is their only option. For some, this restrictive environment is temporary. For others, it is permanent. Thus, **M** becomes either a stopgap measure or a lifelong sexual outlet. Either way, masturbation serves a definite purpose: to relieve sexual frustration and therefore, help keep people focused upon their mission in life (or help them accept their fate).

There are those critics who would quickly posit the rejoinder: Why not recommend abstinence or self-control? This question is a good one, but I believe misplaced. Once it has been established that masturbation poses no mental, physical, or emotional harm to humans, and it is essentially a morally neutral act, then the question of self-control becomes moot. It simply doesn't apply. One need not worry about masturbating if it doesn't harm anyone and is not morally "bad." The self-control factor only comes into play when masturbation develops into an abnormally frequent habit. But again, this signals underlying psychological problems, not that M, of itself, is wrong.

Speaking to the subject of abstinence, we can only applaud its virtue. If members of society promise or choose to abstain from any sexual activity, for some chosen "higher purpose," this is indeed laudable. However, for society to expect a version of sexual abstinence (and in particular, masturbation) would be wrong. First, sex is not bad or evil of itself, but on the contrary, represents natural human behavior when employed appropriately. Secondly, most human beings are not born with nor can they easily develop, a "heroic degree" of will power sufficient to forego a perfectly normal, harmless human behavior by sheer choice.

It is for this reason that we do not universally recommend abstinence with regard to masturbation. Any form of human behavior which can be beneficial to most people without causing any harm to the person or to other members of society is a behavior to be accepted and therefore, protected from moralistic people. Many religious persuasions have labeled masturbation "self-abuse." Quite frankly, one does not abuse oneself by relieving sexual tensions. Rather, to the contrary, someone abuses himself or herself when he or she permits sexual frustration to change their lives for the worse, and alas, visit their personal frustration on others in their family or community.

Masturbation never has and never will have a negative impact on society. The fact that people masturbate, and do so for many reasons including pleasure, has little to do with the continued propagation of the species. The sexual direction of all living things is toward replacing its lost members. Therefore, heterosexual intercourse will forever be the mainstream of sexual activity. The extinction of any form of life is attributable to reasons other than purely sexual. If human life ever ceases to exist as we presently understand it, the reasons for human extinction will have no relationship to M, but have everything to do with the ill advised or wrongful decisions of the human mind.

Every facet of human logic argues to the assigning of value to masturbation. But logical conclusions have not been drawn regarding **M** throughout history. In fact, the continuous development of human understanding plus the growth of scientific and general knowledge has failed to be adequately applied to the act of solitary sex. The upshot of this historical pattern is the ensconsement of ignorance relative to M, and we all know that ignorance breeds fear and distrust, prejudice and bigotry, and summary denunciation. Masturbation has never had a chance to display its role in the sexual history of human life. **M** is not something good; it is not something bad. It is merely a useful tool in the ongoing development of human life.

We conclude here with the words of Dr. Warren Johnson:

> "Students of human sexuality and of mental health are increasingly taking the position that masturbation may be regarded as part of the normal process of development, including sexual maturation, and as a legitimate human behavior at all ages. Lacking health if not societal and legal reasons for combating masturbation, teachers and counselors might best relax themselves about the whole

matter and merely attempt to help the individual live successfully with the existing biological, psychological and sociological realities. It is perhaps a major tribute to the human life force that the most extreme and persistent efforts to eliminate masturbatory behavior--ranging all the way from severe punishment, including death, to sterilization and to special chastity belts--have generally failed. Now that the most diligent effort has failed to produce any evidence of clear and present danger associated with masturbation, a new look at the whole subject seems entirely in order. There seems to be a growing consensus that no one, neither child nor adult, should be subjected to indignities, let alone persecution, for sharing a near universal interest which might, under certain circumstances at least, be encouraged rather than discouraged. Traditional direct or indirect preventive actions have made little or no sense because they have presumed the culpability of the behavior itself. On the other hand, it makes a great deal of sense to help change attitudes towards the behavior, while at the same time helping those in need of social perspective to adjust themselves successfully to the demands of the real world." (Johnson, Ed.D., pp. 94-95.)

BIBLIOGRAPHY

Adams, Carl. Secrets of Marathon Masturbation. New York: Helios Press, 1979.

Atwood, J.D., and J. Gagnon. "Masturbation Behavior in College Youth." Journal of Sex Education and Therapy Vol. 13 (2) 1987: 35-42.

Bakos, Susan Crain. Sexational Secrets. New York: St. Martin's Press, 1996.

Barbach, Lonnie Garfield. For Yourself: The Fulfillment of Female Sexuality. New York: Signet, 1975.

Bausch, William. Becoming a Man. Mystic, Connecticut: Twenty-Third Publications, 1993.

Bechtel, Stefan, and Laurence Roy Stains. Sex: A Man's Guide. Emmaus, Pennsylvania: Rodele Press, 1996.

Block, Joel D., Ph.D. Secrets of Better Sex. New York: Parker Publishing Co., 1996.

Bauer, Alan R., M.D., and Donna J. Brauer. ESO: Extended Sexual Orgasm. New York: Warner Books, 1983.

Buttler, Robert N., and Myrna Lewis. Sex After Sixty: A Guide for Men and Women in Their Later Years. New York: Harper and Row, 1976.

Catholic Theological Society of America. Human Sexuality: New Directions in American Catholic Thought. New York: Paulist Press, 1977.

Cherry, Sheldon, M.D., and Carolyn Runowicz, M.D. The Menopause Book. New York: Macmillan, 1994.

Coleman, Gerald D. Human Sexuality. Staten Island, New York: Alba House, 1992.

Comfort, Alex, M.D., D.S.C. The New Joy of Sex. New York: Crown Publishers, 1991.

Dillon, Valerie Vance. Becoming a Woman. Mystic, Connecticut: Twenty-Third Publications, 1993.

Dodson, Betty. Liberating Masturbation. Union, New Jersey: Sensory Research Corp., 1972.

Dodson, Betty Ph.D. Sex for One: The Joy of Self-Loving. New York: Crown Trade Paperbacks, 1996.

Doress-Worters, Paula B., and Diana Laskin Siegal. The New Ourselves, Growing Older. New York: Simon and Schuster, 1987.

Ellis, Havelock. Studies in the Psychology of Sex. 2 vols. New York: Random House, 1942.

Ellis, A. and A. Abarbanel, eds. The Encyclopedia of Sexual Behavior. New York: Hawthorne Books, 1967.

Fisher, H.E. The Sex Contract: The Evolution of Human Behavior. New York: William Morrow, 1982.

Fisher, Helen, Ph.D. Anatomy of Love. New York: Faucett Columbine, 1992.

Ford, C.S., and F.A. Beach. Pattern of Sexual Behavior. New York: Harper and Row, 1951.

Fossey, D. Gorillas in the Mist. Boston: Houghlin Mifflin, 1983.

Frazer, J.G. <u>Pausania's Description of Greece</u>. New York: Macmillan, 1899.

Friday, Nancy. <u>My Secret Garden</u>. New York: Pocket Books, 1977.

_____,. <u>Forbidden Flower</u>. New York: Pocket Books, 1975.

Gray, John, Ph.D. <u>Mars and Venus in the Bedroom</u>. New York: Harper Collins, 1995

Goldstein, Martin, M.D. and others. <u>The Sex Book: A Modern Pictorial Encyclopedia</u>. New York: Herder and Herder, 1971.

Hacker, Sylvia S., Ph.D. with Randi Hacker. <u>What Every Teenager Really Wants to Know About Sex</u>. New York: Carroll and Graf Publishers, 1993.

Hare, E. H. "Masturbatory Insanity: The History of an Idea." <u>Journal of Mental Sciences</u> No. 452 1962: 2-25.

Hass, A. <u>Teenage Sexuality</u>. New York: Pinacle Books, 1981.

Hayden, Naura. <u>How to Satisfy a Woman Every Time</u>. New York: Bibli O'Phile Publishing Co., 1982.

Hite, Shere. <u>The Hite Report</u>. New York: Macmillan, 1976.

_____. <u>The Hite Report on Male Sexuality</u>- New York: Alfred A. Knopf, Inc., 1978.

_____. <u>Women As Revolutionary Agents of Change: The Hite Reports and</u> Beyond. Madison, Wisconsin: University of Wisconsin Press, 1994.

Hoffman, Eileen, M.D. <u>Our Heart. Our Lives</u>. New York: Pocket

Books, 1995.

Hooper, Anne. The Ultimate Sex Book. New York: Dorling Kindersley, Inc., 1992.

Hunt, M. Sexual Behavior in the 1970's. New York: Dell, 1975. "J." The Sensuous Woman. New York: Lyle Stuart, 1969.

Johnson, Warren R., Ph.D. Sex Education and Counseling of Special Groups. Springfield, Illinois: Charles C. Thomas Publisher, 1975.

Kaplan, Helen Singer, M.D., Ph.D. The Illustrated Manual of Sex Therapy.Sec. ed. New York: Brunner/Mazce, 1987.

Kaplan, Louise J., Ph.D. Adolescence: The Farewell to Childhood. New York:Simon and Schuster, 1984.

Katchadourian, Herant A., and Donald T. Lunde. Fundamentals of Human Sexuality. New York: Holt, Rinehart and Winston, 1972.

Kinsey, A.C. and others. Sexual Behavior in the Human Male. Philadelphia:W. B. Saunders Co., 1948.

Kinsey, A.C. and others. Sexual Behavior in the Human Female. Philadelphia:W.B. Saunders Co., 1953.

Kiassen, Albert D. and others. Sex Morality in the U.S. Connecticut: Wesleyan University Press, 1989.

Kolodny, R. and others. Textbook of Sexual Medicine. Boston: Little Brown, 1979.

Kulliger, J. L. Masturbation: The Art of Self-Enjoyment. Canoga Park, California:Omega Press, 1975.

Kune, Jeffiey, R.M., M.D., and J. Asher, M.D. The American Medical Association Family Medical Guide. New York: Random House, 1987.

Kuriansky, Judith, Ph.D. <u>Generation Sex</u>. New York: Harper
    Collins, 1995.

Kurtz, Irma. <u>Ultimate Problem Solver</u>. New York: Cosmopolitan
    Books, 1995.

Lieblum, S. "Vaginal Atrophy of the Postmenopausal Woman."
    <u>Journal of the American Medical Association</u> Vol. 249. No.
    16 1983.

Locker, Sari. <u>Mindblowing Sex in the Real World</u>. New York:
    Harper Collins, 1975.

Long, James W., M.D., and James J. Ryback, Pharm. D. <u>The
    Essential Guide to Prescription Drugs</u>. New York: Harper
    Perennial, 1995.

Lorben, Judith. <u>Paradoxes of Gender</u>. New Haven: Yale University
    Press, 1994. "M." <u>The Sensuous Man</u>. New York: Lyle
    Stuart, 1971.

Masters, William H., and Virginia E. Johnson. <u>Human Sexual
    Response</u>. NewYork: Basic Books, 1966.

_____. <u>Human Sexual Inadequacy</u>. Boston: Little
    Brown and Co., 1970.

Masters, William H. <u>Human Sexuality</u>. 5th ed. New York: Harper
    Collins College Publishers, 1995.

McCarthy, Barry. <u>What You Still Don't Know About Male
    Sexuality</u>. Toronto: Fitzhenry and Whiteside Limited, 1977.

McCoy, Kathy, Ph.D., and Charles Wibbelsman, M.D. <u>The New
    Teenage Body Book</u>. New York: The Body Press/Perigee
    Book, 1992.

Monat-Haler, Rosalyn. <u>Understanding and Expressing Sexuality</u>.
    Baltimore: PaulH. Brookes Publishing, 1992.

Offit, Avodah K. The Sexual Self. New York: Lippincott, 1972.

Patterson, Ella. Will the Real Women Please Stand Up. New York: Simon and Schuster, 1996.

Pearsall, Paul, Ph.D. Sexual Healing. New York: Crown Publishers, 1994.

Pogrebia, Letty Cottin. Getting Over Getting Older. New York: Little Brown. 1996.

Reinisch, Jane M., Ph.D. with Ruth Beasley. The Kinsey Institute New Report on Sex. New York: St. Martin's Press, 1990.

Renshaw, Domeena, M.D, Seven Weeks to Better Sex. New York: Dell Trade Paperback, 1995.

Ruben, David M.D. Everything You Always Wanted to Know About Sex* but were afraid to ask. New York: Bantam Books, 1971.

Sachs, Judith. The Healing Power of Sex. New Jersey: Prentice Hall, 1994.

Schogol, Marc. "Personal Briefing," The Philadelphia Inquirer 11 February 1997: D3

Stanway, Andrew. The Joy of Sexual Fantasy. New York: Carroll and Graf Publishers, 1991.

Stekel, W. Auto-Eroticism. New York: Liveright Publishing Corp., 1950.

Swift, Rachel. How to Have an Orgasm ... as Often as You Want. New York: Carroll and Graf Publishers, 1993.

"Taking Sides": Clashing Views on Controversial Issues in Human Sexuality. 4th ed. Guilford, Connecticut: Dushkin

Publishers Group, 1994.

Teaff, Nancy Lee, M.D., and Kim Wright Wiley. <u>Perimenopause - Preparing for the Change</u>. Rocklin, California: Prima Publishing Co., 1996.

Van de Velde, T.H. <u>Ideal Marriage</u>. New York: Random House, 1965.

Villarosa, Linda, ed. <u>Body and Soul</u>. New York: Harper Perennial, 1994.

Westheimer, Ruth K., Ph.D. <u>Sex for Dummies</u>. Foster City, California: I.D.G. Books, 1995.

Witken, Mildred Hope, Ph.D. <u>45 and Single Again</u>. New York: Dember Books, 1985.

Zibergeld, Bernie, Ph.D. <u>The New Male Sexuality</u>. New York: Bantam Books, 1992.

About the Author

TERENCE E. TIERNEY was a columnist for Emmanuel Magazine and THE BEACON. He has authored more than 175 articles for magazines, journals, and newspapers in the United States and abroad. In addition, Mr. Tierney is the author of six books, one of which is still selling briskly after more than 27 years. Mr. Tierney's education, legal background specializing in marriage, and his experience as a counselor on marriage and family life enable him to bring a wealth of knowledge to the topic of sexuality. He and his wife of 25 years live in Pennsylvania. They have two sons, one pursuing a degree in journalism, the other a doctorate in educational psychology.